ACTIVE VOICE

ACTIVE VOICE

A Writing Program
Across the Curriculum

James Moffett

SECOND EDITION

BOYNTON/COOK PUBLISHERS
HEINEMANN
Portsmouth, NH

BOYNTON/COOK PUBLISHERS, INC.
A Subsidiary of
HEINEMANN EDUCATIONAL BOOKS, INC.
361 Hanover Street, Portsmouth, NH 03801
Offices and agents throughout the world

Library of Congress Cataloging-in-Publication Data

Moffett, James.
    Active voice : a writing program across the curriculum / James
Moffett.—2nd ed.
        p. cm.
    Includes bibliographical references.
    ISBN 0-86709-289-0
    1. English language—Composition and exercises—Study and teaching
(Secondary) I. Title.
LB1631.M54 1992
808'.042'07—dc20   91-46812
                                                                  CIP

Printed in the United States of America

92 93 94 95 96   10 9 8 7 6 5 4 3 2 1

Contents

Preface to Second Edition

In this edition I have not so much revised the text as added to it to integrate it better into subsequent works. Its present form seems to have worked so well for many individual teachers, preservice courses, in-service programs, and Writing Project institutes that overhauling seems ill-advised. And its unique genesis, recounted within, argues also for preserving its original coherence. But its broad program has always begged for exemplification, and that is what I have added.

This takes two forms. While revising with co-author Betty Jane Wagner the more comprehensive volume, *Student-Centered Language Arts, K–12: A Handbook for Teachers* (fourth edition, 1992, Boynton/Cook), I shifted more than a dozen student writing samples, including my analysis of them, from it to *Active Voice*. Here they serve not only to illustrate certain writing assignments but also to exemplify issues for workshop discussion.

The other form of addition consists of cross-references to anthologies of student and professional writing samples, published since this book first appeared, and of the tables of contents of these collections (at the end of the main text). *Active Voice* aimed originally, after all, to outline a writing repertory across the curriculum, but suffered in this respect from a lack of examples. The problem was that illustrating all the types of writing would have made an impossibly bulky work. Furthermore, samples would have had to be replicated for elementary, middle, and high schools. By referring you to these anthologies, I am able to overcome this problem without adding appreciably to the size of this volume itself.

Indeed, it was specifically to exemplify this necessarily skeletal work that I undertook with various other teachers to compile four volumes of writing for Boynton/Cook, entitled *Active Voices*, the title referring to the student authors. The samples for volume I of *Active Voices* were drawn from grades 4–6, for volume II from grades 7–9, for volume III grades 10–12, and for volume IV from college. *Active Voice* is for teachers; *Active Voices* for students. These collections are subtitled *A Writer's Reader* and are indeed intended as high-interest peer reading matter to launch youngsters into both the reading and writing of the types of discourse illustrated. Each sampling is preceded by the assignment directions that might prompt it—and nothing else. As readers, students not only become familiar with the assignments that make up a writer's repertory, but can see how one type of writing relates to another.

The tables of contents of these anthologies differ somewhat from the array of writing types in *Active Voice*, in ways that readers of this book will appreciate as both rearrangements for the benefit of the students and as refinements permitted by the luxury of greater space. The brief *Rationale and Teacher's Guide* that accompanies *Active Voices* also supplements this book. It explains this alternative way of arraying a writing repertory and suggests various sequences that might be put together from it for different writing courses or for an indiviualized writing program.

The original *Active Voice* cited titles of professional examples to illustrate some of the types of writing. I've updated these "Collateral Reading" sections. The original text also referred to selections in an anthology of short stories I compiled with Kenneth McElheny, *Points of View* (Penguin USA). These references remain. The arrangement of short stories in *Points of View* parallels the development of narrative in *Active Voice* and *Active Voices*. Paralleling all of these in turn is an anthology of professional nonfiction that I compiled since *Active Voice* first appeared and that *Active Voice* now refers to as well. This collection is *Points of Departure* (Penguin, USA). Like its companion volume of fiction, *Points of View*, it suits high school and college.

Another more recent book—the second, augmented edition of *Coming on Center: Essays in English Education* (Boynton/Cook)—carries further some lines of thought about writing and treats the broader verbal and social context of it. *Student-Centered Language Arts, K–12* elaborates this writing program within the framework of all the language arts. Its companion volume of theory, *Teaching the Universe of Discourse* (Boynton/Cook), places the language arts, in turn, within the perspective of overall total discursive education. These broader contexts are important, because a book about writing alone risks violating the integrity of total learning. With these internal additions and external contexts, *Active Voice* should continue to prove useful to writing teachers, who are, after all, nearly always teaching other language arts and, of course, the whole person as well.

ACTIVE VOICE

Explanation of the Program

BACKGROUND

A word first about the history of this program, since many people in the field have known and used it in an unpublished version that I devised only for experimental purposes while teaching at Phillips Exeter Academy during the early 60s. Though a mere one hundred copies of this version were run off on a mimeograph machine, I was repeatedly startled during my travels around the country to encounter either these copies themselves, now a good fifteen years old, or fresh printings of them, sometimes retyped or even revised. Originally I had slipped copies to just certain teachers or supervisors I knew who wanted to try them out or were developing a new curriculum. I never expected that form of the program to endure, nor intended to publish such a version.

Even after I did publish similar assignments mixed with other material in *Student-Centered Language Arts and Reading, K-13* and as activity cards in the *Interaction* program, some people kept following and distributing the old version. A number of these people helped to start or worked closely with the Bay Area Writing Project, and so they handed out copies to project classes around the country. I was both pleased and concerned. I knew that the likes of Jim Gray, Keith Caldwell, Cap Lavin, Mary K. Healy, and Ken Lane understood and shared my reservations about the old experimental program and would modify it accordingly—and I have joked with them about disseminating an underground, unauthorized version—but at this point its continuance holds risks for both new users of it and for me. It attracts some people for the wrong reasons and misleads others about what sort of curriculum I've been proposing.

Understandably, many teachers are looking for something that looks like a syllabus so they can seize on it and apply it directly to their classroom. A neatly numbered sequence of directions to the students with some operating instructions for the teacher creates a powerful temptation. Many users of the original simply started in with number one and tried to do the whole sequence in a year—the unit of time that naturally dominates most teachers' thinking—whereas I was dealing with the whole span of school years and expecting any one teacher to

3

try out only a certain segment or selection from the sequence. The predictable result was that hardly anyone ever reached the later assignments, which featured exposition and argumentation, and the program acquired the reputation, especially among those who were merely hearing about it, of not treating "ideas." What a painful irony for me, since thinking processes formed the very basis of the whole sequence from first assignment to last, and I had tried very hard to show how *all* writing expresses ideas, regardless of mode, and how the higher abstractions teachers look for in familiar essay form derive in stages from lower abstractions formulated more personally and fictionally at first. But so few teachers ever got beyond informal, dramatic, and first-person writing that this intellectual development was lost, and my work sometimes became inappropriately identified only with informal, "personal" writing. Part of the problem here is that many in the profession still don't acknowledge ideas except when the writing is about books or teacher-made topics, whereas we should all know that writing about books and teacher topics does not guarantee thought or hold a monopoly on thought. At any rate, later assignments included precisely the explicit "idea" essays that teachers so concerned are looking for. Actually, what the sequence really lacked was more opportunities for poetry and other imaginative writing, which the present version offers. It was precisely the emphasis on logical development in the original version that caused me to slight poetry. In publications aiming for completeness, as the unpublished program did not, I have given poetry the big play it deserves.

Getting stuck at the earlier range of the sequence was not the only problem teachers created who did not understand the experimental nature of the original version. Some found that sensory writing or interior monologue, say, came too early for their students. They were not alone, but instead of seeing this discovery as part of an experiment, they reacted as if the program were a published guide. And others who never tried the assignments rightly saw from experience that the order of certain assignments might cause problems and criticized publicly what was never offered publicly. But this takes us back to the problem that has necessitated the present publication, namely, that this old work now enjoying currency in the national writing movement (and sometimes called The Exeter Exercises) is misleading and needs to be replaced.

Well, what are the differences between the versions? I'll answer at first by dealing with what they have in common that justifies any new version at all. The original purpose, which still holds, was to *enunciate* writing assignments important enough to become central in an English curriculum and to *array* them in an order devised to induce insights into composition, language, and literature. Such an order was to correspond as nearly as possible to mental growth over a long span and, over a short span, at least to practical strategies for learning one kind of discourse through experience with another (e.g., written through oral, monologue through dialogue, narrative through diary, first-person fiction through real autobiography, and so on). Emphasis was on, and remains on, the evolution of one kind of discourse into another, on progressions of assignments that allow language experiences to build on and reinforce each other in significant ways. I now believe, however, that sequencing en masse can occur only grossly over a very long haul and that specific sequencing—day-to-day and even month-to-month— should occur on an individual basis. More on sequence later, but for now it's enough to say that though much of the original order remains, it shouldn't necessarily be followed as a writing order as before, when I recommended skipping assignments at the teacher's judgment but not reversing their order. Publication requires commitment to *some* order, and the sequences found in this book (several now, not a single one) remain valid in their demonstration of relations among different kinds of discourse even if not practiced in the order presented.

GENERAL DESCRIPTION
OF THE PROGRAM

The original assignments as now modified have in this version been broken down into three groups to be regarded as running parallel more than as lying end to end. They are *Revising Inner Speech, Dialogues and Monologues*, and *Narrative into Essay*, each of which will be more fully described later just preceding the assignments representing it. In brief they are:

1. Basic-source kinds of pre-composition writing that can lead to many different sorts of finished products—note-taking on one's spontaneous inner speech to garner material to develop.

2. Dialogues leading to monologues, based on the development of the ability to sustain monological continuity out of the give-and-take of conversation.

3. Narratives of increasing distance between author and subject, blending into essays and articles of generalization and argumentation.

I have added some new assignments to include valuable kinds of writing often paralleling or preparing for the old ones as well as standing quite worthily alone. I have described these assignments much more briefly because I think that the exposition of the three theoretically related groups will enable the reader to place these in a context and to apply the same classroom processes to them. Elementary teachers may find an especially large number of assignments among these that will be suitable for their students.

Most of Groups One and Two, and much of Three, can be done in elementary school, but don't risk underestimating students; include in your program any assignment that *some* students *might* do. All the assignments are appropriate for secondary school and most for college as well. Except for some near the end, they can be done with varying maturity at different ages. I have stated most directions so as to indicate where students derive the content from and how they abstract it. For younger students these may often have to be cast in a catchier way. Try things out, interest other teachers so you can trouble-shoot and brainstorm together, and do the assignments yourself!

In this program of writing assignments, the student is asked to draw subjects from actual personal observation and to abstract this material in ways that: entail increasingly sophisticated and artful decisions; assume a more and more remote audience; lead from vernacular style to literary style, from improvisation to composition; and open up for the student progressively higher realms of abstraction. The program would teach much more than is normally understood by "writing" or "composition." This teachers' guide sketches ways in which the writing produced in response to these assignments may be used to explore many issues usually placed under the heading of language and literature. Part of the purpose of the program is to teach such things as grammar, punctuation, logic, semantics, style, rhetoric, and esthetic form through writing and workshop discussion of the writing. Essentially, this is a functional, global approach that, instead of subdividing English into blocks of content, would teach most aspects of the subject, including aspects of literature, simultaneously and interrelatedly, through examining student productions side by side with analogous professional writing.

The "Collateral Reading" sections indicate which kinds of works might be read in conjunction with the different writing assignments. A degree symbol (°) by a title means that that selection can be found in *Points of Departure*; an asterisk (*) indicates that it is included in *Points of View*. Part of the purpose of the program is to teach comprehension of drama, narrative, poetry, and essay through writing.

This guide is general, not a rigid step-by-step lesson plan. It describes each assignment, explains the purpose of it, relates it to other assignments, suggests what the teacher and the student might do with the papers in class, identifies the main issues raised by each assignment, and sketches some lines of workshop discussion. The program is flexible and contains many options along the way. Participating teachers may select as a class repertory a segment of the sequence that seems appropriate for their students or "strip out" a series by skipping over certain assignments.

Many of the later assignments are long. The whole philosophy of the program demands such length. This is not a particle approach based on writing "exercises"—a sentence, then a paragraph, then a double paragraph. In fact, it challenges such an approach and insists that only within some whole, actual discourse based on individual thinking can words, sentences, and paragraphs—or style, rhetoric, and logic—be meaningfully practiced and examined. Furthermore, a claim of this program is that students are more highly motivated to write realistic discourses grounded in the writer's experience. Untold damage has been done in the teaching of composition by asking students to cover too much in too short a length. It is essential to set a good ratio between the scope of the content and the quantity of wordage. Otherwise the writer is forced to overcondense, a malpractice that results in exactly the faults teachers complain of—dryness, lack of detail and development, and obscurity. Dealing with the large quantities of writing necessary for a good writing program calls for an unconventional classroom management whereby students as well as the teacher process the writing. The fact is that a teacher alone cannot process the quantity of writing students need to do to get good at it. If you limit the amount to what you can "correct," you become a bottleneck—an awful thought for any serious teacher. Just because a teacher feels drastically overworked does not mean youngsters are writing enough. This is one of the reasons I advocate small-group writing workshops and other classroom practices discussed further on.

SEQUENCE

No bigger snare exists in curriculum than the one of sequence. Educators often fail to make some key distinctions. One is between sequence based on whatever we can ascertain as a biologically programmed growth schedule (Piaget's concrete to logical operations, for example) and sequence based on some "reasonable" exposition of the subject matter (deduction in the new math or chronology in history) or perhaps just on local expedience and legal requirements (myth in the 9th grade because so-and-so knows myth and teaches the 9th grade, or American literature in the junior year). In other words, many sequences may have nothing to do with how people grow. Sometimes this disconnection will make the difference in curricular success or failure, and sometimes it will make no such difference (because students have already acquired whatever competence the order requires). In the original, experimental version of this program I was trying to find out what differences the given order made, that is, when it seemed necessary and when optional, which is the difference between growth order and a merely utilitarian sequence.

Over the years I have concluded that my original sequencing, which I still offer but with modifications, has value for deciding roughly which kinds of writing to offer at very different ages. In a talk to the New York State Education Department Conference on Writing Education, David Dirlam said

> Advances in writing research over the last decade and a half have provided significant knowledge of the natural design underlying the development of writing ability. James Moffett provided a comprehensive theory of discourse development which analyzes discourse into levels of audience, subject, viewpoint, logical sequence, literary form, continuity, word selection, and syntax. This theory has received extraordinary empirical support from the studies of James Britton in England and from my own work.[1]

But this correspondence to growth is not fine enough to warrant a claim for any span of time so small as a year or even two. Put another way, individual differences in growth rate and growth order outweigh, over such a short time, any universal sequence or timing. You can't *generalize* for a whole peer group about anything so *specific* as what kind of reading or writing its members' growth demands by the middle of eighth grade, or which assignment has to be done before another within a six-weeks period. So often when I tried to set a lower grade limit on an assignment I found that at least *some* students below that grade could do that assignment. Fixing one sequence for all constantly risks underestimating what people can do and hence holding them back, because commitment to a universal sequence forces us to rule certain assignments in or out for a given grade and to require that assignment X be done before assignment Y, whereas I often found that some fourth-graders could do what some ninth-graders could not and that some youngsters could do very well a certain assignment without first doing other assignments that I thought would be prerequisite.

So the second key distinction contrasts group sequence with indi-

---

[1] "The Changing Wisdoms in Children's Writing," May 22, 1980 (unpublished article). See J. Britton, T. Burgess, N. Martin, A. McLeod, and H. Rosen, *The Development of Writing Abilities, 11–18*, Macmillan, 1975 (available from NCTE).

vidual sequence. When educators speak of sequence, I find, they virtually always mean for a group and most often for a year, whereas I believe we must regard individual sequencing as the *order of the day*, with which most teachers would be routinely involved, and regard group sequencing as valuable only in contemplating the main articulations between primary, elementary, junior, and senior high. Long-range, universal development can help us decide which arrays of writing to offer during these major phases from which individual sequences may be made up. We should keep in mind also that most assignments here may be usefully repeated cyclically over the years because increasing maturity and experience naturally make something new out of them each time. The fact, however, that an assignment can be valid for different maturity levels should not be made a reason to assign to a whole class the same assignment at the same time. Such procedure still thwarts both the individual's motivation and the teacher's wish to treat the resulting papers as the same assignment for all, because to the extent the students' responses differ, it is not the same assignment.

We would do well, also, to regard any sequence of writing assignments as an *accumulating repertory* from which nothing is ever really dropped. Growth means being able to do more things and to do old things better, not merely hopping from one stepping stone to another. The time at which youngsters become ready and willing to do a new kind of writing varies so much that only an extremely general group sequence will not conflict with individual needs. This is so because a myriad of local and personal factors determine readiness and willingness besides the universal biological ground plan, which individual organisms manifest differently anyway. Teachers need to be prepared for much overlapping between the array of writing offered in one year or one school and that of the next. If, for example, we reserve the writing of "Generalization Supported by Instances" or "Interior Monologue" for secondary school, we will surely be making an adverse decision for those elementary children who can rise to the challenge. If sequencing is individual, then it harms nothing to *include* those, since other, unready students will not be saddled with them. Too often sequencing has acted negatively on learning by placing unwarranted and unnecessary limits for the sake of standardization. We must not reduce public education to the standard of the least developed. Similarly, insisting that every student write "Thematic Collection of Incidents" before "Generalization Supported by Instances" may not make sense or be necessary for some students: they may have achieved the *cognitive* prerequisite of "Generalization" by means of other experience than writing, or they may have a better reason to do "Generalization" *now* and may in the course of doing it work *back* to or fall back on "Thematic Collection."

These considerations lead to a third worthwhile distinction between sequence for the student and sequence for the teacher. That is, assignment progressions may serve to aid teachers in thinking about many practical issues in teaching writing whether or not their students write in the order of the progressions. In this respect, I hope this volume will prove useful for in-service experience. Even at the outset it was intended for that, and Writing Project directors and supervisors have often testified that having teachers write some of the assignments and discuss the assignments makes for good teacher education in composition. The spirit of this program remains somewhat experimental in that teachers can use the assignments and the commentary on the assignments as a way of finding out for themselves how to make decisions about what their students should write and what teaching methods work best.

Even if students do not do all of these assignments or do not do them in the order presented here, they will be working within a framework that will enable the teacher to relate whatever they do write to other assignments they have not written yet. Contrast, for example, the array here with a miscellaneous listing of assignments. A miscellany is not bad, but a presentation that interrelates assignments according to basic communication structure and principles of verbal and conceptual growth should help the teachers see useful connections among various sorts of writing and make a whole in their minds of this variety. This in turn should help them assess relative difficulty and appropriateness for different kinds of students and thus run an individualized writing program and small-group writing workshops or even run better a more traditional program.

The main progressions may be summarized as follows:

1. From vocal speech and unuttered speech to private writing to public writing.
2. From dialogues and monologues to letters and diaries to first-person narratives to third-person narratives to essays of generalization to essays of logical operation.
3. From an intimate to a remote audience.
4. From vernacular improvisation to literary composition.
5. From immediate subjects of small time-space scope to remote subjects far flung in time and space.
6. From recording (drama) to reporting (narrative) to generalizing (exposition) to theorizing (argumentation).
7. From perception to memory to ratiocination.

8. From present to past to potential.
9. From chronology to analogy to tautology.

The sequence is by no means just linear, however. I've tried to spiral it by, for example, dealing with idea writing in dramatic and narrative modes long before it is fully treated in the expository mode. It's easy to say that growth goes from informal to formal, personal to impersonal, and lower to higher abstraction, but it's not easy to know what these progressions really mean and entail. I've tried to interweave progressions and to interrelate discourses in such a way as to illuminate growth in practical terms of writing activities.

All this does *not* mean that formal or more impersonal or more abstract writing is better. The goal of writing through such a spectrum is not to "come out on top" but to be able to play the whole range. As applied to abstraction, "higher" and "lower" are not value terms but refer, rather, to stages of symbolizing that people progress through as they become *able*, but not *obliged*, to discourse at further removes from the here-and-now. I've tried to show that every stage of writing has its own value and that writers of whatever maturity return to earlier stages over and over. Making up stories, for example, is obviously a very sophisticated, mature activity, since it comprises most of literature, which is regarded as a major index of civilization. Some kinds of writing such as dialogue become incorporated into narrative or expository prose. Sensory recording of what one saw or heard is summarized and recast and then assimilated into a larger piece, as in reportage.

My efforts to delineate a discursive spectrum corresponding to growth has often been misunderstood as preferring the upper end of the spectrum, as if our job were to hustle children up a ladder. It's not our job to prefer. Our job is, again, to enunciate and array assignments. I have merely sought to bring into school the actual kinds of writing practiced outside and to offer them in a coherent way relevant to how people learn. "Here's God's plenty—go to it" is the intended spirit. We should *enable* youngsters to abstract at as high a level as they are capable of so that they have maximum range and choice, but this goal does not at all imply that they should abandon kinds of writing they learned earlier. Not only do we return in many ways, but every authentic writing activity can be done at many levels of maturity.

Finally, this sort of effort to ensure practice across the whole discursive range naturally entails "writing across the curriculum," to use the phrase American educators have adopted from Britain and have rightly made an issue in curriculum development. It means teaching writing as practiced in all disciplines by teaching it through all the school subjects. Because the assignments in this book are based on

Schema of Discourse
(reading down)

Progression of Speaker-Audience Relationship

Thinking to oneself	Inner verbalization
Speaking to another person face to face	Outer vocalization
Writing to a known party	Informal writing
Writing to a mass, anonymous audience	Publication

Progression of Speaker-Subject Relationship
(subject translated into verb tenses)

Recording what is happening	Drama	The chronologic of on-going perceptual selection
Reporting what happened	Narrative	The chronologic of memory selection
Generalizing what happens	Exposition	The analogic of class inclusion and exclusion
Inferring what will, may, or could be true	Logical Argumentation	The tautologic of transformation and combination

various first- and secondhand sources of knowledge, they naturally include both the processes and the products of science and history—observation, interview, notes, logs, reportage, chronicle, source documents, generalization, and syllogistic reasoning. For fuller development of the whole discursive spectrum and of its translation into disciplines or subjects, please see *Teaching the Universe of Discourse,* where I defined history, science, and philosophy as different levels to which we abstract experience. In this view, literature is a figurative mode spreading across a wide range of the spectrum but of another dimension because literature *simulates* abstraction in the literal mode, as fiction simulates true stories. For further description of this developmental approach to writing in particular, see the essay at the end of this book, "I, You, and It."

These writing assignments externalize thinking processes—how people conceptualize and synthesize their accumulating experience. That's why the concept of abstraction is central. Abstracting is distilling. A student who writes down everything she is aware of at a given moment, selects out later some perceptions or memories or reflections, then writes these up as a composition for a purpose by organizing them according to *previous* abstractions now constituting her current frames of reference, is recapitulating in writing what goes on all the time anyway in our mental processes.[2] The progression drama-narrative-generalization-argumentation describes not only long-range growth toward an enlarging repertory but describes also the daily abstracting we do as we convert new experience to working knowledge. Inwardly, we record or register the drama of our ongoing perception of what is happening in and around us, file a report on this to our memory banks, where it is assimilated and consciously or unconsciously organized according to classes or categories derived from society and past experience. The mind formulates new generalizations or confirms previous ones based on these classifications and combines these generalizations to infer a system of interlocking propositions that constitute our outlook and that will act downward in turn to influence how the next experiences shall be registered and digested. Writing reflects inner mental structures.

Writing also taps the virtually unceasing stream of our inner speech. To compose is to focus rather drastically this stream, select and edit excerpts from it (about any subject matter whatsoever), and order it according to our innate abstracting faculties. What composition teachers call "coherence," "organization," and "style" are manifestations in writing of mental functioning. These assignments thus mimic key features of the abstracting process we use every day to symbolize accumulating experience. A diary summarizes the events of each day but recounts these events without the retrospection of a later vantage point in time when they would usually "look different," that is, become assimilated further into a more generalized summary. "Thematic Collection of Incidents" replicates in its very form the mental act of classifying, as "Arguing a Theory" does the act of syllogizing. This paralleling allows the teacher—and eventually the student too, we hope—to relate coherence, organization, and style to their inner sources and hence better to the practicalities of writing. Compos-

---

[2] In this book, the gender of pronouns alternates.

ing words on paper, in other words, is viewed as what it really is—composing the mind.

And yet these assignments are just directions for producing common kinds of writing actually practiced all the time outside of school. I worked backward from an examination of the discourse our world turns out as items in magazines, journals, and newspapers or as whole books or other printed matter. Some writing that may look artificial at first, like jotting down sensations or memories, is a form of note-taking of the sort professional writers do all the time. It is a pre-composition sort of writing and not at all artificial. It's merely a stage toward another form that will be the finished product. Just as more comprehensive stages of abstracting incorporate and digest simpler ones, so later kinds of discourse in this book subsume earlier ones. Consider a writer utilizing X's autobiography and others' memoirs of X to write a biography of X—as well as X's use of his own letters, diaries, etc. to write his autobiography in the first place. The assignments aim to combine the realities of inner functioning with the realities of society as reflected in the kinds of writing actually practiced in the world for which school is preparing children.

CLASSROOM PROCESSES

The descriptions of the assignments assume certain classroom processes but limit themselves to the kinds of issues a writing workshop discussion would engage with. They do not deal with how groups form or operate. Similarly, those descriptions imply or assume other kinds of writing or pre-writing activities that might precede the writing assignments but they do not go into them. What follows is a synopsis of processes *assumed* for the assignments. If you're not familiar with some of them, you'll need to supplement this sketch with reading elsewhere and experimentation.

Since doing the first version of these assignments, I have come to advocate individualizing the assigning of reading and writing, wherever possible, rather than expecting a whole class of 20–40 people to be ready and willing to read or write the same thing at the same time, which strikes me now as unrealistic and self-defeating. In *Student-Centered Language Arts*, K-12, Betty Jane Wagner and I set forth in some detail how to go about running a classroom in which different working parties of learners do different things at the same time, sometimes alone but most often with a partner or in small groups, so that individualization is balanced with interaction. I can only sketch the processes here.

Keep a display of all the possible writing assignments available to students, preferably in the form of activity cards bearing directions and of wall charts summarizing and perhaps relating assignments, as in this book. The *Active Voices* anthologies array and exemplify the full repertory for students and give directions. Activity cards may be school-made and can refer to materials, reading selections, and locations accessible to students. Part of the secret of individualizing is to route students around in a set of materials especially set up to array choices and to facilitate self-direction as much as possible. Part of the rest of the secret is to devise your way of keeping track of what kinds of work each student has already done so that you can size up what experience he or she has been logging and what he or she might benefit most from next.

Periodically, look at an individual's record, look over her collected written work, and have a conference during which you can ask questions to learn further what she has done and perhaps make suggestions about which direction to take next in writing. All papers accumulate in a folder or box bearing the individual's name. By the time the writing settles into the folder you'll be familiar with most of it from seeing it posted, witnessing it being performed, reading it in a booklet, hearing it discussed while sitting in on a writing workshop, being involved in pre- and mid-writing stages of it, and so on. Perusing the whole of someone's writing for a marking period, you have a chance to pull it all together in your mind, to spot traits and trends that tell you what to give as a grade, if one is required, and how to counsel the student. From the folder, you and/or the student may select papers for various portfolios for evaluation or other purposes.

What will also facilitate individualizing is small-group work. Partners help make decisions and figure out and carry out directions. Partners also pool knowledge and understanding of everything from spellings to life experience. Partners raise morale, spread responsibility, share and balance emotions, and provide social satisfaction until successful experience has shown the inherent satisfactions of writing. Most difficulties teachers can foresee occurring with individualization will eventually work out through a combination of prepared materials, small-group process, and the freedom that this increased self-direction affords you for circulating around the classroom and working with groups and individuals.

Learning to write occurs best if the composing process is spread out into several phases that a student goes through in writing something. The assignments of Group One, *Revising Inner Speech*, establish this clearly, but there are other ways of staging befitting other kinds of writing. One stage may be the gathering of new material prior to any writing, as in research. Another may be talking over early ideas with partners or a "coach." Not all stages are pre-writing; talking over one's ideas in mid-composition or after a draft is often extremely useful. Various kinds of responding to the finished product—forms of audience feedback—constitute a stage too, since learning the effects of what one has written on one occasion serves on other occasions.

It's, of course, entirely possible, though not recommended, to approach these assignments conventionally by having all students do them at the same time and in the order given and by leading the whole class yourself as a single group. Even if you do this, it would be best to stage the composition process more or less as indicated below, because the real learning takes place from experiencing the *processes* of pre-writing, mid-writing, and post-writing. From these experiences will issue the best *products*, because doing an assignment will teach, not merely test.

Please understand that the use below of the terms "pre-writing," "mid-writing," and "post-writing" is strictly a convenience for describing different cycles of composition, all of which have value for their own sake.

Pre-Writing

Coming up with a subject, a reason for writing about it, and a form to write in can often happen rather naturally for individuals in an integrated language arts program where writing is going on in close conjunction with dramatic activities, work in other media, and reading in literature and other areas. A so-called pre-writing activity may simply be another activity done entirely for its own sake—a discussion, improvisation, slide-tape, consumer-research project, experiment, interview—for which some composition seems, in retrospect, a good follow-up. Parlaying one good activity into another helps make individualization work really effectively. Decisions about which kind of writing to do next can be made with an eye to a student's total work and can be worked out between teacher and student in varying degrees of direction by the teacher. (Treating students differently is part of individualizing.) Playing by ear like this becomes much easier if you array in advance the materials and processes that you will implement.

Needed Knowledge

Let's assume now that some choice of writing assignment has been made. Pre-writing activities for it will depend on the nature of the assignment and some may have been done while doing a previous activity. Garnering knowledge is prerequisite to many assignments based on writing from fresh material and doing firsthand abstracting. There are four main sources of information outside of oneself:

- What the environment shows. (Witnessing.)
- What other people know. (Interviewing.)
- What records store—books, films, tapes, etc. (Researching.)
- What experiments prove. (Experimenting.)

The last allows one to find out what is unavailable from any of the other sources.

There are four main sources within oneself:

- What invention constructs. (Imagining.)
- What memory stores. (Recalling.)
- What logic infers. (Reasoning.)
- What intuition reveals. (Meditating.)

The last simply involves concentrating intently on, or visualizing, some object, emblem, or idea that stands for the subject one wants to penetrate and understand better. Imagination rearranges reality as logic recombines ideas, both to get at and beyond the mere evidence of the senses. So as regards the gathering or utilizing of material, pre-writing will consist of one or more of these eight activities. Composition begins with purposeful choices of what to write about.

Some "pre-writing" is, strictly speaking, *pre-composing*, being itself some kind of writing. One could also regard it as a draft, but it really comprises notes or a write-up of notes to keep a record, say, of what the interviewee said, what ideas came out of brainstorming or discussion, a dream one had, observations made during experiments or while visiting a site, information from a book or film, memories or thoughts, and so on. In a program like this, one composition may itself be the basis of another. After summarizing a journal of observations made periodically of a certain activity, for example, an author might incorporate conclusions or instances from the journal summary into an article. A narrative might later be subsumed as instance or evidence in an essay of generalization.

Oral Dialogue

Partners may talk over and plan together what they think they will try to say in their composition. Even novices can help each other foresee some problems, get good additional ideas, and think through what one has in mind. These may be the same partners as will respond to drafts later, in which case they will know what the author set out to do and what some of her problems were. Or a discussion of a book or issue begun for another reason may send participants rushing off to continue the discussion on paper as a more effective way of crystallizing and expressing their views. Or students may improvise a scene orally first, as recommended in the assignments for "Dialogues and Monologues," before improvising one on paper in script form. A group might improvise several versions of a scene and do a take with one by writing it down from memory or transcribing it from tape. Talking is, after all, the main form of pre-writing (especially if one includes talking to oneself, inner speech).

Oral Monologue

Let's say that a child is showing and telling about a certain object. If she does this in a small group and listeners know to ask questions if they have them, the teller will learn what her audience wants to know that she did not at first include. Now she is ready to write something about her object, drawing on her practice run and feedback. The same happens for a youngster narrating or explaining a set of slides or photos she has taken (or pictures she has drawn or an exhibit she has put together). After orally improvising once or twice, she will arrive at an improved version that she can then write down definitively as a composition and perhaps record to make a slide tape or "talking exhibit." In fact, any early composition effort can be done orally and extemporaneously to a group who can ask questions or otherwise react. Thus, one could tell a memory or dream or explain how to do or make something, garner reactions, and then plow the benefits into a written composition, perhaps using a tape recorder as a memory aid. Listeners might later react also to the written version. Some students might prefer just to talk into a recorder without an audience, then edit and revise as they transcribe, at which point they might ask a partner to listen and react with them.

Reacting to Professional Compositions

This is a well-established practice. Students view photos, paintings, or films, or listen to music or other prepared sounds, and then write thoughts, feelings, or stories that are thus elicited. Sometimes writers write about what they've read—react to others' ideas or imaginative creations. The compositions may be taken from any medium; the purpose is simply to stir up material in the writer to draw on in her own composing. Keep in mind, however, that another composition is already an abstraction or symbolization of experience and may overinfluence the novice. Plagiarism or borrowing is far less likely to occur when writing about a composition in another medium. The real problem arises when teachers chronically require students to write on assigned books, to find out if they read them or understood what they were supposed to.

As I hope the array in this book demonstrates, writing about books is only one very limited and (outside of school) rather rare kind of writing. (It comes down to one variant of "Generalization Supported by Instances.") Many other kinds require at least as much thinking, and often more, with less chance of students having their own thinking short-circuited by reworking or repeating others' abstractions. Using writing to test reading amounts to a terrible abuse, because it has monopolized composition instruction in this country to the exclusion of writing that develops greater range of technique and more independent intellectual activity and that would lead ultimately to better critical writing as well. I fear some teachers have been deceived by the *apparent* abstraction level of student essays about books. The level looks high because the student is manipulating ideas someone else has already done the real abstractive work to formulate.

Mid-Writing

After a writer has done some version of her composition or begun to put together some material she has collected, it's often helpful to get advance audience reactions while changes can still be made, to have an opportunity to use questions and other responses to prompt further thoughts about what one is trying to say and how best to say it. Anyone can serve as a kind of coach. Responders may be other members of a working party whose separate writings will all go into a final project, a temporary partner or two, other members of a writing workshop group who have been together some time and are familiar with each other's work and have developed trust, or, of course, the teacher, who by sometimes working one-on-one and sometimes sitting in on a project party or writing workshop can set a tone and furnish a model of good responding. You might want to introduce a kind of writing new to most of your class by presenting and leading discussions of samples from a former class or from *Active Voices*. Members of workshops may read aloud their own papers, read aloud each other's papers, or read papers silently; they may make comments orally one-to-one, during discussion, or as written marginal notes.

How to Respond

Responding to someone else's writing seems most effective when it comes as the natural reaction of an authentic audience. We should not be in a hurry to make a blanket judgment. Remember that being helpful to someone in mid-task is the key. We don't have to play critic and act teacherly. Here are several alternatives that should become habits for students to pick up from you.

1. *Describe* what the piece seems like so far and the impressions you had at various points as you read or heard it. Reflect directly the mood, idea, or effect conveyed to you. Most often writers can get from this a very strong idea of how to revise or proceed in a final draft, because they know what they were trying to do, so that even if you make no suggestions whatever for improving the piece, you have in fact helped them see what to do.

2. *Ask* the author questions that occur to you. The author can decide if she wants these questions to arise in the reader's mind. Questions may be to clarify something puzzling, to corroborate an impression you have, to see why the author did this or did that at a certain point. Or, in the playback spirit of 1 above, you can ask questions to check if your understanding or response gibes with what the author intended.

A good combination of describing and asking will often cause the author to think out unresolved problems of composition or even to think further through the original ideas and perhaps reconceive a main point or line of argument or organization. As the work of Donald Graves shows in elementary and Adela Karliner in college,[3] this role of eliciting, of getting the author to begin revising already while she is talking with you about what she wants to say, can have extraordinary benefits for both the final version and for future writing. Mid-composition dialogue may be the best way to help a writer externalize and revise her inner speech toward an audience.

3. Let the *author ask* questions about what she wants responses to. This encourages her to acknowledge what she's worrying or wondering about in what she has done so far. She can say what she was trying to do and ask if it worked. Or she may want help sizing up the possibilities in material she has come up with so far—journal entries,

---

[3] For the latter, see Suzanne E. Jacobs and Adela B. Karliner, "Helping Writers to Think: The Effect of Speech Roles in Individual Conferences on the Quality of Thought in Student Writing," *College English*, January 1977.

surveys or interviews, research in records, or jumbles of memories. Direct suggestions for the next steps are more appropriate now, if the author has asked for them.

4. Take a *what-if approach*. Help the author test out what she's got so far by seeing what difference it would make if you changed this or that—added or deleted something, reordered some things, shifted emphasis, and so on. Doing different versions of an improvisation—altering factors such as time, setting, relations, tone—sets a good model for this. While stimulating creativity, this approach also may help an author see weak places without feeling criticized. Removing something is a good way to find out if it is needed, and rearranging a sequence of images, ideas, events, or paragraphs can show splendidly many aspects of a composition that may need to be brought out, if only to be appreciated.

5. *Make up a title* for the piece under consideration. An effective procedure that can be used routinely begins with the author committing herself at least provisionally to a title but writing the title on a separate slip of paper, not on the draft. Without knowing this title, responders each make up a title after reading or hearing the draft, write it on a slip, and reveal these one at a time. They discuss how well each seems to fit and then compare these titles for how widely they scatter or cluster. Then they compare all with the author's title. A tight cluster shows a sharp coherence or clear point. A wide scatter may show a number of things, all useful or interesting: the piece may work at several levels, or evoke different but warranted personal reactions, or be incoherent or ambiguous. Students also learn to work with a title as a guide to unity and intent and to invent good titles over a range of sorts—direct-label, poetic, humorous, ironic, metaphoric, and so on. Authors are free to use a suggested title or keep their own.

6. For certain kinds of writing a *special test* or *audience* makes sense. If students write stories for younger children, they can try out drafts on a few samples of their target audience. Directions for how to make something can be tried out by others and revised according to problems encountered. Scripts can be run through also to spot needed changes.

Small Groups

The teacher's job is to make available as much useful response as possible during phases of composing and to establish a model of reacting. Although response can often be arranged ad hoc according to need and circumstances, it can be institutionalized somewhat by making small-group work a staple process. Writing groups may be of all sorts:

1. A good initial experience for undeveloped writers may be *collective writing*. Two to five students choose to write one composition together by taking turns scribing as all utter ideas and formulate sentences. This combines pre-writing with composing and revising, since all go on in the same session. Ideas are offered, weighed, tried out, changed, and parlayed into further ideas. Spelling, punctuating, and paragraphing are thrashed out together by pooling understanding. Ideas are committed to writing but may get changed later as the composition develops. This collaboration will teach an enormous amount about how to write, build up confidence and interest, and prepare for solo writing and the workshop process.

2. Members of a *writing workshop* may come together only for one session because they all want to do the same kind of writing at the same time. Or they may stay together for weeks or months and enjoy the benefits of increasing trust and familiarity. Experience with both, concurrently or not, is important. Members choose, perhaps with the teacher's help, an assignment to write separately but share afterwards. For certain long assignments having several stages, they might meet more than once. The size of the group depends on the experience of the participants (start around three and go to five), on the length and complexity of the assignment when meeting only for it, and to some extent on the chance readiness and availability of individuals. The composition of the group may be by acquaintances (at first), by a careful mixture of talents or personalities on the part of students and/or teacher, and again by readiness and availability.

The teacher sits in or overhears to tune into what members are helping with or not. The following write-ups of assignments usually indicate much of what to expect as composition issues in each case (and you should stay alert to how different assignments raise different issues). You have to recognize these and other issues in the form *students* will encounter or raise them and perhaps translate into terms you know how to deal with. Note what kinds of exchanges and interactions are going on and try to replace negative or unproductive ones by those listed above. Here, if anywhere, it's true that example is the best teacher.

3. The project of a whole class or large group may require that subgroups write up or write on different aspects of the project, which might be consumer research or a magazine or newspaper or *Foxfire* type of publication comprising a variety of contributions. Members of subgroups might be writing collectively or individually but would in any case meet from time to time to coordinate efforts and help each other toward their particular group contribution. This could mean that they act as editors for each other before some final editing of the whole

project. Prior experience in the groups described above would certainly make this editing both more effective and less unsettling for authors.

Post-Writing

If the first cardinal rule is "Give students some real choice of assignments so that they want to do them and you can be sure that any problems will result from true compositional difficulties, not from poor motivation," the second cardinal rule is "Put writing to some realistic use after it is done, and make clear in advance of writing what that purpose and audience are." Assignment descriptions and directions should stipulate purpose if it's not distinctly implied there or elsewhere. Writing for a grade or for compliance only is not enough of a real reason to establish an authentic rhetorical relationship and ensure relevant motivation. But the assignments themselves must be authentic ones practiced out of school. If they're only exercises, you won't be able to find anything to do with them afterwards that students can recognize as realistic.

Three things to do with final versions of writing are *post, print*, and *perform*. Some short pieces, especially if based on pictures, make good browsing when posted on classroom or hall walls. A good writing program requires generous use of printing facilities. The booklets turned out by students become reading matter. One excellent reason for including script writing and directions is that they have a very definite function—to be carried out or enacted—that readily leads into the next activity. *Dialogues and Monologues* are clearly written to be performed. Whether on a regular or impromptu basis, allow plenty of class time for groups to make presentations to the class of what they have written. Some groups can, of course, perform scripts written by others.

Allow time also for other kinds of sharing—perusing posted material or reading printed compositions. *Narrative into Essay* assignments could mostly be printed and passed around. Interesting possibilities are to print like assignments together—fragments of autobiography or how-to-make directions—or to mix discourse in a magazine-type booklet or to mix fiction only or to put out a booklet all by one person. Seeing each other's work encourages students to try writing things they would not otherwise consider, and reading writing produced from an individualized classroom becomes a substantial education in itself, because classmates are introduced, in effect, to a greater variety of kinds of discourse than if they all write the same thing. You'll seldom see students throw away a copy of class writing. It's a fact that students writing for a real audience and purpose often will amaze you by how fast they clear up some old "writing problems." Most printing should include everybody's writing, not be limited to contest victors. Both performing and printing, in fact, should be staple classroom procedures.

Some casual writing like diary entries may be shared by talking about them in small groups, extracting from them for other writing, or summarizing as another composition. Letters may actually be mailed or delivered. A story written for younger children can actually be read to them in or out of school. The more out-of-class audiences the better. Many of the assignments in this program lead to reportage, case histories, chronicles, and feature articles that local newspapers or other publications might really be glad to have. Some teachers go to great lengths to establish connections between classroom and community publications or outlets and are well rewarded by the vigorous interest this arouses in students for writing.

Post-writing activities, then, should give writing as satisfactory a recompense as possible and at the same time provide further feedback, from a larger or different audience, about the effects of what one has written. Both benefits will transfer to future writing.

Assignments

Group One
REVISING INNER SPEECH

Inner speech verbally distills some ongoing stream of consciousness. All writing has to be an edited and revised version of the inner speech someone produces at a particular moment under the influence of random or controlled circumstances. Both talking and writing may be usefully regarded as a revision of inner speech, talking being more spontaneous and writing more pondered. The second group of assignments will deal with the composing of vocal speech. This group replicates in writing the whole shift from inner speech to outer speech that occurs continually as people verbalize their experience for others. It is designed to show students how to tap off and verbalize what is going on at any moment in their sensations, memories, thoughts, and feelings. Since this inner speech reflects outer material and may be about any subject, impersonal as well as personal, notations made of it may be composed into any kind of discourse for any purpose. This recording is the matrix, then, from which any kind of writing may develop and can be done by any person of any age or capacity. Some teachers lump this with "free writing," but I don't because that term has a specific meaning for some people, such as an open-topic composition or formless final paper, whereas I distinguish those from the noting of what spontaneously comes to mind, which is the basis of these assignments.

The first five of these assignments could be given at any age after the student has mastered handwriting and spelling enough to be able to write sustainedly for fifteen or twenty minutes, although, of course, the wording of the assignment and the kind of discussion that should ensue are matters to be modified according to the teacher's judgment and experience. The last two assignments, featuring reflection, will probably be inappropriate for most students under ten or eleven.

These first seven assignments establish the base for all kinds of writing that might be taken up later—dramatic, narrative, expository, and poetic. They do this by helping the student to: find material readily, put himself at ease with the act of writing, develop an eye and ear, distinguish between improvisation and composition, distinguish be-

27

tween writing for himself and for others, become aware of how his verbalizing apparatus works, note the difference between his perspective and that of others, become sensitive to form and function in actual operation, and accustom himself to using the process of feedback and revision.

An all-important act must precede writing. It is *witnessing*. People are forever witnessing and composing meaning out of what they witness. This group of assignments puts this dual process into writing. We witness both outer things and inner things, according to where we focus. Writing both requires self-awareness and induces self-awareness. Deliberate concentration is essential. These assignments build a method of sustained concentration followed by composition.

Stream of Consciousness

For fifteen minutes write down, pell-mell, everything that comes into your head, using the first words that occur to you and without concerning yourself about grammar, spelling, form, and continuity. This should be a kind of fast note-taking to get down as much as you can of what you think, feel, and sense during those fifteen minutes. No one else will ever see this, but it will be important for later work.

The purpose of this assignment, best done at first in class, is manifold: (1) To limber up the student and make his writing fluent and natural; (2) To show him that there is plenty to write about if he just becomes aware of what is going on in and around him; (3) To anchor writing in honest, original interaction between him and the world; and (4) To provide a sampling of his own verbalization which he may subsequently examine to learn about the putting of things into words.

You might take students through the first round of this kind of writing as a whole class, then let them repeat it on their own as individuals or in small groups.

Begin by asking students to close their eyes, sit straight but very relaxed, take a couple of slow and deep breaths, and try to stop thinking for a minute or two by releasing thoughts along with muscles. Afterwards ask how well they succeeded in not thinking for even that short a time. Ask those who say they did succeed what method they used. Give the class a chance to air this experience, then give this assignment as an invitation to just go ahead and *let* the thoughts come, to witness them and catch as many on paper as possible. Do it with them, and refer to things you notice about your own paper as you lead discussion of theirs.

The only audience for this kind of writing is the author, but it is done in company with others, at first at least, and an unusual kind of valuable sharing can occur if you put a number of questions to the students just after they have finished. What they have written are notes on their witnessing of their own mind. Now they compare notes. Notes are the writer's fodder, the first draft of something yet unknown. By questioning them as they look at their papers, you may guide them by remote control through an analysis of many verbal, compositional, and semantic issues that later assignments will afford opportunities of following out. Ask them first what it felt like to do this kind of writing. Was it difficult? If some say that they went blank, ask what happened instead and how they got going again. If some say that they couldn't write fast enough to keep up with their thoughts and feelings, ask how they decided which to put down and which to leave out. This quickly gets into the crucial compositional matter of what determines our spontaneous choices. If some say, "I put down what was most important or interesting," ask what standard of "important" or "interesting" they were going by, since the assignment indicated no topics or values or audience. Did they find themselves, despite the directions, trying to stay on a subject, find a continuity, or move toward a goal? If so, why? As you will find as you ask some of these and the following questions, beginning in a private verbal chaos has the great advantage of letting the student discover for himself the reasons and ways for moving toward form, communication, and a public universe of discourse.

Ask them to look over their paper, mark the different verb tenses they have used, and say which tense, if any, dominated. If they don't know the grammatical terms, use this occasion to teach them. Past tense indicates memories; the future and conditional, perhaps wishes, anxieties, conjectures. Distinguishing between the progressive form of the present, which records ongoing action, and the present tense of generalization is an effective way of distinguishing sensory data from "ideas." Have them label the contents of their paper by writing "sensation," "memories," "emotion," "fantasy," "reflection," and whatever other labels they think appropriate over the top of the original writing. Such distinctions are not only useful for the setting up of later assignments but also make students aware of the mixture of material and sources in their inner speech.

You can point out that the dominant tense is one index to the focus of their thoughts when they were writing; some students might have fastened on the surroundings, some on the past, some on a dream world, and some on anticipation of coming events. Tell them to ask themselves how characteristic this sampling is of their thinking all the time and how much it reflects present circumstances. This kind of awareness may be personally helpful to many students, and they are generally interested in this analysis because it is of their own production, although it obviously touches on universal issues.

Some questions that direct their attention to form and grammar are: Did you use whole sentences or fragments? What kinds of words were most dispensable—what parts of speech? Did you paragraph? If so, why? (What kind of logic determined new paragraphs?) Did you punctuate? Since no one else was going to read this, what purpose could it serve? What did you use dashes and commas for? Does your paper jump; that is, could someone follow from one part to the next? What would prevent them? In a month, would you be able to follow it yourself? Does it have any particular beginning or end? Do you hear more than one voice in this paper? From whom or what do the voices issue? What attitudes or feelings do they represent? How do the voices interact with each other? Where do *you* stand among the voices?

Then comes the crucial question that pulls many of the previous questions together and that gets to the heart of rhetoric: What would you have to do to this paper to make it, first, *comprehensible*, and second, *interesting* to someone you know (get a definite person in mind). After they have thought this over and give some answers aloud, ask what it would take to make this paper comprehensible and interesting to a large, public audience. They should consider everything from word choice and punctuation to complete reorganization and reformulation of the content. Ask who thinks they have the makings of a good composition there and what kind of a piece of writing it would turn out to be. Encourage them to go ahead and write that. Suggest to the others that they do this again in other places alone until they have some material they want to work into a composition.

Of course, it might be best to repeat this assignment in class several times and bring up only a few issues each time, perhaps repeating some. You'll certainly think of other questions and may develop your own way of raising issues and discussing them. If the class gets at least a working understanding of how our inner stream of consciousness breaks down roughly into sensations, memories, and reflections, the ground work will be laid for other assignments: sensations are the base for description and recording; memory for narrative; and reflection for essay. Images and emotions seem to play in and over these strands rather than to constitute their own strand, or, at any rate, verbalizing them in more than flashes seems impossible for most people; but they are very important and must not for this reason be allowed to get lost. Different kinds of writing can emerge by tapping different currents of the inner stream and catching the feeling that rides along with them.

Spontaneous Sensory Monologue

Choose a place away from school that you would like to observe, go there with paper and pencil, and write down for fifteen minutes what you see, hear, and smell. Think of what you write as notes for yourself later. These notes will be used to write something, to be decided later, that will become part of a booklet. Don't worry for now about spelling or correct sentences; write in whatever way allows you to capture on paper what you observe during that time. You may also include your thoughts and feelings about what you observe. You may also want to say what things look, sound, or smell like.

A great deal of experimentation has been carried out with this assignment from fourth through twelfth grades and much learned about its many possibilities and problems. Since it would take disproportionate space to do justice to the varieties and ramifications of this key assignment, I urge the interested reader to consult pages 215–24 of *Student-Centered Language Arts, K-12* for reportage of some trials, for more detailed suggestions, and for discussion of actual student papers. Here we will touch briefly on major points.

Ongoing noting of observations turns the focus of witnessing to outside things, but this deliberate narrowing of the inner stream is not meant to break connections between what one sees and what one feels or thinks about what one sees. "Observation," we note, has the double meaning "registering externals" and "commenting." It is the *associations* one has or makes to the externals that motivate writing externals and that make one person's observations interesting to another. "Pure" observation doesn't exist, since the act of perceiving begins itself the process of composition—of selecting, coloring, and ordering. While raising this whole issue, the assignment does aim to help youngsters become better observers and shape their personal responses to the world in a way others can share.

However true it may be that younger children are more limited to the here-and-now, experiments make clear that *verbalizing* and *writing down* sensory impressions are difficult for them. Observing for its own sake is a rather mature activity. Children are more inclined to *look for* than just to *look*. Writing up random observations takes sophistication. The less developed your students are, the more strongly would I recommend that you provide a context and reason for the observing and the noting. The directions given above start at a level of motivational development and maturity enabling students to go out of school to a locale of their own choice. They can pretend to be reporters or detectives or may derive plenty of motivation from feelings and associations they already have about the place. And feeling *is* the key. Younger children will have to observe plants or pets in school or places you take them on field trips. Whatever the material, it must *already* appeal to them because of prior associations and feelings. Arbitrariness, we found, is the real enemy of sensory writing. If you make the choice of what to observe, you must know the children very well to ensure that they will want both to observe and to write about what you choose for them. Keeping a class log of periodic observations of the same thing or place can be a good beginning if all take turns making entries. But introduce individual choice as soon as feasible.

It's very important that the focus on sensory material does not cause youngsters to screen out feelings and thoughts, since this too will reduce interest. Experiments showed that memory writing always went over much more readily than sensory writing, at least as the latter was first set up, because memories already mean something and are remembered precisely because of feelings and associations one has about them. Memory, furthermore, composes experience by its own process of selection and classifying. By comparison, sensations do feel much less meaningful and much more raw—unless observing is embedded in a situation that gives looking and reporting meaning.

Many interesting variations of this assignment are worthwhile. One is to take one sense at a time. Tactile riddles can be made, for example, by having one person write down what a partner says he feels while blindly handling objects in a bag. Writing down only sounds automatically produces a narrative, since sound does not occur without an action. Other variations are to write down observations in very different kinds of places—quiet and noisy, with and without people, open and enclosed, urban or sylvan; in the same place at very different times—sunny and cloudy weather, morning and evening, busy and empty; or any place in company with classmates. Variations open up rich possibilities for what to do with papers afterwards and give students more choice of material to compose into finished pieces.

Workshop Issues

Since sensory recording seems rather impersonal, it's possible to discuss some papers in class before turning subsequent discussions over to workshop groups. It may be necessary to introduce sensory monologue to a whole class, to acquaint students with it, before putting it on a basis of individual choice.

The assignment especially invites us to distinguish between sensations and personal responses, and this effort will teach a lot, but it should never appear to students that you're implying they were wrong to note nonsensations. The main thing is to become *aware* of how much one is mixing in feelings, inferences, or judgments. Even "It's a fine day" is a judgment. Copy or project a few papers and ask what words or phrases or statements express things other than sensations. Have students underline these in their own papers and write in the margins whatever labels they think appropriate for these nonsensations. "Loaded" words and phrasing can come under scrutiny but only if made to appear as positive possibilities rather than as mistakes. Nonsensations may be clues to how to make a composition from apparent miscellany, because they indicate a mood or attitude or idea that might be a natural unity or focus to compose around.

Responders can also try to picture for themselves where the observer was and what action was going on, what the time and weather were, and what the relations are among items mentioned. You might get this going by asking questions about what they think the scene is (and about how the observer reacted to it). What comes through the observer's way of selecting and noting? If a group of students has observed at the same locale at the same time, a sometimes fascinating discussion may occur as these papers are compared. This comparison usually shows dramatically how differently individuals see the same things or select from the same scene or say what they see. Students will learn from this how personal are perception and the verbalization of it and why people have difficulty communicating or agreeing about what seem to be "objective" and "external" things that "any fool can see."

Call attention to the *form* of the notes. Ask students if they wrote down everything. How did they decide what to leave out? How did they try to abbreviate the writing so they could get down more? Lists or telegraphic phrases increase coverage but lose detail, whereas full sentences retain detail but probably omit more items. Authors of the papers discussed can say what they left out and why they used the form of noting they did. What form allows the writer to recall more detail later but doesn't take too much time while he is observing?

Composed Observation

Choose one of your sets of sensory notes and rewrite it in any way that you think will make it more understandable and in-

teresting to certain other people. Feel free to add, subtract, rear-
range, reword, or do as a poem. You can distribute it to whoever
your audience may be.

This assignment makes clear the distinction between private improvisation and public composition. The student should come to understand that spontaneous note-taking has great value for getting
material down in a fluent first draft, but that such material, so treated,
cannot be expected to be of value to an outside audience until that
audience is taken into account through revision. This assignment is
supposed to produce a finished piece. It might be wise to have the
younger student pitch his paper to a personal audience: ask him to
write it as he would say it to a friend, or as a letter to someone, or as
an entry in a diary that he would read years later. The important thing
is that he have a firm sense of *some* kind of audience whose interests,
knowledge, and background he must take into account. Of necessity,
he will have to conform to some universal understanding and expectations about grammar, structure, and word usage.

A key strategy in this whole program is to put students in a position
of writing from plenty rather than from scarcity. Instead of facing blank
paper and a bare topic and having to strain for something to say, the
student starts off with a problem of selecting out—composing or
abstracting—that is easier to deal with and educationally more to the
point. It is not hard to jot down some notes pell-mell. Add to this other
sets of notes from other occasions, and you have real riches. The problem becomes not how to get an idea (scratching the head) but which
possibilities to develop (plucking the nuggets). Add further to this that
one has partners to keep choice from being overwhelming, to help see
what one has got already and what may be done with it. It will often
happen that students will at first feel they need many sets of notes to
choose from, fearing they are poor, but will later go back to unused
material and see many other possible papers.

Sensory composing, furthermore, is the proper way to get detail into
student writing. Teachers constantly nag students to be more specific,
to illustrate, and to put in more detail to "make it real," but usually
we work at this from the wrong end. ("Putting in" detail gives away
the problem.) We work *deductively, down* the abstraction hierarchy
instead of starting students off where the detail comes from—
observation—and having them abstract inductively from notes of details up to higher orders of writing.

Workshop Issues

Point out possibilities you see in papers for a composition and ask students to look at their own papers with an eye to plucking out a nugget or selecting a few things that seem to make a whole or perhaps using the bulk of the material as is. Workshop groups should spot opportunities and help members see how they might write a finished piece from their notes. Sensory notes can go in virtually any direction—reportage, story, descriptive sketch, idea essay, poem, or play. An observed locale could become the setting for a made-up story. An overheard conversation could become a script for a play scene. Observed activity could prompt general reflections for an essay. By example, help students see the possibilities for parlaying their initial perceptions into something much extended—or to recognize good material when they already have it and need merely to shape it a bit. Most observations are not pure miscellany but have some viewpoints or motifs or focuses that can be brought out. Ask students to spot these in each other's papers. (Often the author may not be aware of how much he has already started composing.) Look for threads. Ask students if they see a continuity even if it is interrupted. Good descriptive reflecting to an author of what his material seems to contain or be about will often suggest how to proceed.

Sensory monologue provides an excellent lead into the writing and reading of poetry. Make sure that students learn to include in their cross-commentary suggestions for making a poem out of certain material that turns up in classmates' writing. Point out possibilities yourself, and introduce sensory poetry to them for reading. The figurative nature of poetry makes it tend to be sensuous. Many poems feature an object, plant, animal, scene, human drama, or other "subjects" that could be perceived or witnessed at a certain time and place. Many other poems, though more abstract, keep touching on the sensory world through allusions, comparisons, and other imagery. Poets often get an idea for a poem by simply watching or listening to something with great concentration. Then other images and ideas come. Even if these take the poem out of the scene through imaginative extension, they still owe their place in the poem to the initial sensory observation. In Group Four are directions to write Haiku and Picture Poems. These are the kinds of poems most obviously related to this assignment, but keep in mind that sensory observations may provide a departure point for many other kinds of poems as well, including narrative as well as lyric. A well-observed place could become the setting of a story, or trigger strong emotions and associations and thoughts, or cast a mood or spell over the observer.

After workshop groups have helped each other settle on certain material and how to shape it, they can serve again to revise the first drafts of these pieces. Copy or project several samples of composed sensory monologues along with the sensory notes they are based on. Ask the class to point out the changes the authors made. Pick samples containing different amounts of rewriting but definitely include some that illustrate a considerable departure from the original. Ask what they think each author was after in the final form, judging from the nature of the changes. Exhibiting stages in the composing process in this way may help novice writers considerably to envision just how much they may do and how many possibilities they have. What idea of the author seems to have determined the way he selected and ordered items, began and finished the piece, and chose his words? The ensuing commentary can then be matched against what the author declares he was trying to do, and also against the original paper on which this one was based. If the piece is a still life, why is such and such item mentioned before such and such other item? What ties them together? What if the order were changed? Which items are emphasized or referred to several times? What did he add, and why? Is there a tone or attitude behind the description? All the problems of writing physical description may be dealt with here. If the scene was active, does the paper tell a story? Follow a chronological order? Have a point? Many issues of narrative writing may be dealt with here, such as use of paragraphing for breaks in time and space, relation of action to idea, relation of action to description, and style and attitude of narrator (does he include himself in the narrative?).

You might also introduce the use of titling as a workshop method if you have not already.

Collateral Reading

Since final compositions could cover a wide range of discourse, there is no single sort of reading matter that exactly corresponds. Haiku and other poetry focused on a moment, object, scene, or living being in a here-and-now fashion would be appropriate. Sportscasts resemble very closely a spontaneous sensory monologue though uttered in more complete sentences. A great deal of single-visit reportage would go well here to represent more selective accounts than the blow-by-blow rendition. You might read aloud or point out to students Lindbergh's *The Spirit of St. Louis*, which is a kind of ongoing record of perceptions, like astronauts' accounts. Various sketches and mood pieces found in newspapers and magazines will parallel many students' final compositions. See "The General Goes Zapping Charlie Cong" by Nicholas Tomalin° and the student samples in *Active Voices*.

Spontaneous Memory Monologue

Look around at your surroundings until something you see reminds you of an event or person or place from your past. Write that down. Now what other memory does the first one remind you of? Once you get started, keep writing down your memories. Write in whatever way captures them quickly. Don't worry about their being jumbled in time or about spelling and correct sentences. Jot down all you can get in about fifteen minutes. These notes will be used for writing something else later. For now it is better to jot down a lot of memories than to go into detail about any of them.

This assignment has been extremely popular wherever tried between fourth and twelfth grades, no doubt because the material is charged with personal meaning. Memory is such a rich storehouse of experience and knowledge that anyone who learns to draw on it for writing knows that he always has something to say that he wants to say. Memories can be about anything one has encountered, not just one's own doings. Because memories are unique they tend to interest others. After all, we read to know what others know, not what we know already. Observations and memories constitute the main personal experience upon which all good writing is based. But this is so because our thoughts and feelings work over raw experience. So much of the process of composing memories centers on how to bring out the thoughts and feelings that frame or invest memories with meaning. This necessarily involves the classification system and particular associations of the individual, so working up memories for an audience helps the student learn something important about his own thinking.

Memory monologue is another special focusing of inner speech. It can usually be easily started by looking around, so wide is anyone's web of associations. Demonstrate for the class yourself by saying aloud what memories come to your mind from looking at a certain object, say what other memory the first recalls, and so on. Then have students do this on paper. Tell them that if a train breaks and they get stuck, look around again until they find another departure point.

Since these papers may be too personal for most students to be able at first to share, discussion might again be by remote control and could proceed along these lines: Did all of your paper cover one time and place? Many times and places? Are the memories in chronological order? If not, how do you explain the order they *are* in? Can you follow all the connections? Could someone else follow the connections? What would have to be made clear in order for someone else to follow? If you cannot make the jump yourself between one memory and the next, take a big step back and try to imagine what the link is. Are all your predicates, if you used any, in the past tense? (They should be, just as in sensory monologue they should be in the present.) Are the sentences not in the past tense, memories? How would you name the material that is not memories? If possible, students might begin to distinguish clear-cut *incidents*—events that occurred on just one day or so—from pervading situations or habitual occurrences. Do you see some single memory or thread or cluster of memories that might be written for an audience?

At this juncture consider several possibilities:

1. Deploy the class into workshop groups to let members talk with each other about what kind of memories and memory patterns they came up with. They can extend lines of examination you started and read or retell certain memories they want to share. Their purpose can be to discover if they have something good there to write further about. Questions and reactions from partners allow them to feel out what might interest an audience. Individuals then do a blow-up of the material by writing down pell-mell everything they can remember about it. In other words, before actually composing the memory they do another memory monologue focused exclusively on the material they selected out, the purpose being to recall as much detail as possible. They might do this in class or at home, then might again meet with their group to share these and make suggestions about how to shape this blown-up material into a final version.

2. Individuals take their first paper home, select alone a memory or memory cluster to compose, and then do a blow-up. They can then bring this to their group for reactions or go ahead and write a draft of the composed memory itself. The difficulty with individuals going off and doing several stages alone is that they tend to move too soon into the final stage and don't get the full benefit of expanded detail.

3. Skip the middle stage of blowing-up and let students take material from the first paper and go right into a draft of the composition either with or without group reaction to the memory notes.

4. Talk one-to-one yourself with individuals to elicit further details. Listen to their initial memories or whatever they care to share with you of them, then say what you'd like to hear more about. You can

draw out detail by asking "Then what?" or more specific questions based on the memory so far.

Which option or combination of options one should play depends on maturity, writing experience, and group experience of the students. Willingness to revise relates very directly to the sense of both an immediate audience like the workshop group itself and of an ultimate, larger audience for which the workshop is helping to prepare the memories. Thinking out loud with a good listener also acts as a powerful stimulus to revise.

Of course, as with sensory writing, let students do the first stage as often as they need to get material they feel is good enough to work with. One suggestion that can come out of groups is that an individual do another Spontaneous Memory Monologue. While helping students to see all the possibilities in raw notes, we also want to keep them from getting stuck with something they can't work with. Photographers take many pictures before they get a few they are satisfied with. And if a student writes down memories while in several different settings, he may find interesting connections between the present and the past which he can exploit later.

You might introduce memory writing to a whole class and then let it go to groups, or you might just start off one group at a time as individual students seem ready for it. Once introduced generally, most groups and individuals can repeat all or some of the process without you. Make clear that memories are a source one returns to over and over, so you are showing them what they may repeat periodically.

Composed Memory

On the basis of your memory notes, write a memory composition that you think will make your material comprehensible and interesting to the rest of the class or some other audience you may choose. Feel free to add or subtract material, to rearrange and reword. This can be printed and distributed, recorded as a reading, or included in a letter.

It might help to launch workshop discussion if you choose a few final papers to look at with the class along with the notes on which they are based. Besides raising some of the following issues, you can ask the authors and their workshop partners to comment on how the composition got from notes to the full draft. Sometimes it's enlightening to present the full or final version first and then the notes, simply asking students what they observe happened between. With the blow-up, you would, of course, have three stages to trace and compare. You might also pick samples with an eye to displaying some of the compositional variety that can come out of memories, as mentioned below. Learning how differently other students did the assignment is of great value to each student: he can see what was or what was not unique in his way of going about it, and can also increase his repertory of possibilities, expand his horizon. Of course, stating the possibilities beforehand would not have at all the same impact or value.

If you wish, you can use discussion of these papers as a way of establishing classifications that may be useful for later narrative assignments and for reading. Does the paper feature the author herself (autobiography)? Does the author share the focus with others, perhaps as a participant in the action (memoir)? Or is she a mere observer, a bystander (eye-witness reporter)? Aspects of style, tone, and attitude can be approached by asking if the students can feel a personality or a point of view behind the writing. Are there particular words or phrases that hint at these things? Or does she state what she feels directly?

Memory writing was the first of several activities introduced to a group of African Americans just out of the eleventh grade who were chosen for their educational promise. The teacher[4] wanted his students to have a chance to write about firsthand material in their own language without worrying about mechanics and right answers, to become involved with their own writing and that of others. Initially, they were unwilling to write at all and virtually unable to talk about writing. For them, composition had always consisted of grammar and rules for mechanics.

Putting down spontaneous memories, expanding and revising some of them, seemed eventually to open them up and get them going. All the memory papers of his sixteen students were surprisingly full—considering that six of the sixteen could not produce at all for a long time. On each other's papers they wrote very helpful suggestions about rephrasing, adding and deleting information, clarifying passages.

SAINT BILLY VISITS AT 9:00 P.M.

Several years ago when I was just a little girl my cousin Vernistine and I lived with my grandmother. I was about nine years old. My cousin was twelve.

Mother told Vernis there was a man who collected all bad kids at night. Vernis replied, "I don't believe you!" Mother said slowly—"all right, I'll see." Vernis disbelieved her. This Vernis had to see with her own eyes. Later mother said, "Since you don't believe me, write him a letter and put it outside somewhere."

Late one evening Vernis wrote the letter. Vernis ask, "Callie, come go with me." Without asking any questions I followed her to put the letter on the bank of the lake. After delivering the letter, we came back to the house; however, Vernis cracked jokes with Mother. "There is no Saint Billy!" Mother replied, "Yes there is—you will see tonight! Saint Billy always knocks three times before coming into a house."

About nine o'clock we heard three loud knocks, and the front door open. Saint Billy walked into the room and said, "Good evening." I looked back and there was an ugly, undescribable man standing in the door. I started screaming. I cried for about one hour or more. Vernis was down on her knees calling on God.

Saint Billy ask, "Can one of you dance or sing?" We replied, "No Sir." He said frightening as he pull a sack from his pocket, "I'll get one of you tonight." I screamed louder and louder, "Make him go away!"

My grandparents laugh until they cried.

Later Saint Billy gave up and went home or somewhere. I was so glad. I don't ever want to see him again.[5]

Workshop Issues

These can be read aloud, exchanged for written comments, or both. In some cases, if the student is willing, it might be worthwhile to also read aloud the preceding paper on which this one is based and compare the two; examining a student's composition process provides a good opportunity to see what he was trying to do and to decide if his judgment was good.

Again, discussion of these papers can explore many issues of nar-

[5] For samples by younger students, see pages 359–65 of *Student-Centered Language Arts, K-12*, which also gives more detail on memory writing.

rative but, this time, in the light not of sensory selection but of memory selection, which is apt to be more inner and closer to the realm of ideas. Papers that are felt to be boring or pointless probably suffer from not *enough* selection, or from lack of any emphasis, or from omission of thoughts or ideas necessary to make the memories meaningful. Some papers, on the other hand, may editorialize at the expense of detail and vitality. Some will be sheer narrative, some will try to make a point applying beyond the specific material. Some will cover one time and place (an incident), some will string separate but sequential incidents into a story, and some will juggle time and relate the incidents in some other way. If time order is disarranged, what other order replaces it?

Since this assignment results in autobiography, memoir, reportage, "Thematic Collection of Incidents," "Narrative Illustrating a Generality," and perhaps other later assignments in this book, the workshop suggestions set forth there would apply here too. Remind workshops too that memories can make fine poems. Suggest too that memories may be fictionalized by making up part of the material and by altering facts.

Collateral Reading

The kinds of discourse just mentioned all furnish relevant reading that you can point out to different students according to the kind of discourse each wrote in. Much personal essay as well as autobiography comprises memories, and all first-person fiction purports to be memory. In the light of their fresh experience selecting, expanding, and shaping memories, it would probably interest many students to consider *Treasure Island* or *A Farewell to Arms* as if they were actual memories (both being told in first-person). Many other things must have happened to these two narrators during the time covered by the book, not to mention the time before and after. What determined what they did tell and what they didn't? Why did they begin the story where they did and end it where they did? What do they tell about directly in detail, and what do they merely refer to or summarize? (That is, what do they emphasize?) Once students grasp just how much the narrator is selecting and editing his memories, they begin to understand better what he is saying as he is telling.

Spontaneous Reflection Monologue

Get alone in a very quiet place and focus as intently as you can on something you want to understand better or think through.

At first close your eyes, sit very relaxed but straight, take several very deep and slow breaths, and shut out all sensations and thoughts about things other than your subject. If the subject of your thought should be a physical object or place, put yourself in its presence if possible and gaze at it. If you have an object or picture that stands for what you want to think about, start gazing at it after you have got very relaxed. If you want to think about something not physically represented, visualize it with your eyes closed, or focus on whatever image or thought represents it. Whether gazing or visualizing, don't try to think but, instead, let the thing you're focused on fill your mind until thoughts about it simply come to you. Stay physically relaxed and breathe easy. Jot down the thoughts in fast note form when it seems right to start writing. Stop writing when it seems to interfere with your thoughts; or write only when you've had so many thoughts that you need to note them to preserve them; or if forgetting does not seem a problem, write your thoughts after you have finished. Whenever your thought train seems to get off your subject, bring your mind back to your focal point. But give yourself a chance to be sure that the thoughts are indeed off the subject and not perhaps a welcome new viewpoint or aspect of your subject. Eventually put down on paper all of the thoughts you have in this session that seem at all likely to be relevant. The more the better as you sort these out later and compose them into some essay to be conveyed to an audience you choose.

This assignment has been considerably modified from the original, which either ended up the same as "Stream-of-Consciousness," because students trying to jot down random thoughts found they had to mix them with sensations and memories, or else it simply did not work, because students found it too difficult to filter out thoughts only. This new version differs considerably in starting with a specific focus for the thoughts. Whereas in a random stream, thoughts constantly interact with sensations and memories and tend to lose meaning without them, in this approach sensations and memories crop up much less often and tend to be more germane when they do. This assignment affords practice in concentrating, which is indispensable for writing and invaluable in many other pursuits as well. It's something that people get better at with experience. Try it yourself on a regular basis and see if it does not teach you a lot about thinking and the control of inner speech necessary for writing. It works only, however, if the subject to be focused on really means something for the concentrator. It's not the straining to get an idea that usually takes place when someone attempts to write about someone else's topic. When it's working at its best, this assignment fuses intellect, imagination, feeling, and experience together into an unusually powerful state of mind from which deeper and more original thoughts emerge about the subject than one could have by ordinary head-scratching cogitation. It should be done several times in order to work out the method a bit and also to be sure to have plenty of choices for composing later. Then, of course, the method should join a permanent repertory of writer's devices.

Workshop Issues

Some outer speech would be most helpful at this point, before further writing. Members can take turns talking from their notes—doing a kind of oral run of what they might write, mentioning problems they may be having, asking listeners what they think of this or that. Appropriate discussion here would emphasize the ideas themselves more than the form of expressing them. This is an author's chance to think through what he has in mind and pull his ideas together by bouncing them off others. Does he have one subject here or several? What would a good working title be? Does he feel that several thoughts belong but doesn't know how to fit them in? Sometimes asking where the main idea or ideas came from helps the author unearth an origin useful for him to know even if not always relevant to include in his paper. This may also indicate how borrowed or original the ideas are. People should know where their ideas come from, and often the origin makes an interesting opening for an essay—something that happened to the author or something he heard or read or witnessed.

Composed Reflection

Rewrite your reflection notes in a way that will communicate your ideas to some audience of your choice and that will interest it. Feel free to revise drastically and to illustrate with real or imaginary examples. Plan to convey this paper to your audience by any appropriate means.

The purpose of this assignment is to let the writer incorporate into a full draft whatever he developed during the previous workshop session and to work up his ideas into an essay.

Workshop Issues

By one means or another an author should find out if his ideas are coming across and interesting others. A major issue always in generalizing is what order of sentences and paragraphs the author has found instead of time order. Would it make a difference if they were switched around? Do responders have trouble understanding because they need more illustration or some background the author has not yet included? Missing links are often a chief issue. Do the ideas seem to need some kind of evidence to support them? If so, what kind of evidence? Or is the paper offered less to persuade than to express personal opinion? These papers will range across several kinds of essays, and group members can determine how each is best taken. They may be humorous or serious, personal or impersonal, commentary or argument. Many poems could come out of this assignment, and the workshop should keep eye and ear cocked for such possibilities. Authors revise in varying degrees, as indicated and impelled.

Collateral Reading

Relevant reading is suggested in the essay assignments that follow, but an especially good source would be the kind of armchair essays that columnists do for newspapers and magazines, not the specialized columnists but the ones who write on any subject of general human interest that occurs to them, often taking off from some event or object or item of information that has crossed their path and made them think. The particular things that prompt their thoughts are the objects of the concentration focuses of the preceding assignment. Many poems, too, like Shelley's "Ozymandias," or Karl Shapiro's "Auto Wreck," are thoughts prompted in the same way.

Group Two
DIALOGUES AND MONOLOGUES

These activities consist of creating scripts and transcripts by making up or recording vocal speech. They put into writing the stage of human development when we make the transition between the give-and-take of dialogue to the more difficult sustained soloing of monologue. Since this progression replicates the whole shift from oral speech to writing, it treats directly the key issues of all other writing, which concern how to generate, clarify, and order one's thoughts once deprived of the collaboration, prompting, and correction of interlocutors.

All oral conversation, including improvisation and discussion, provides pre-writing activities, and transcribing spontaneous speech provides fine practice in "basic" or literacy skills, i.e., spelling and punctuation. Making up dialogue deals splendidly with both reasoning and fictionalizing, since vocal exchange may take a direction into either dialectic (dialogue of ideas) or drama (social interplay), depending on the emphasis of assignment directions and personal inclination. Scripting is a flexible learning means that can very effectively teach many aspects of writing and discourse—more than teachers yet appreciate. It is a familiar gateway to the less familiar domain of expository writing. Published transcripts and scripts provide a wealth of prime reading material crossing all subject areas and spanning utilitarian to literary, intellectual to emotional.

I have reversed here a progression found in the original version. Before, I went from interior monologue to dramatic monologue to dialogue, following the discursive development from private, unspoken thought to social, vocal interaction. That major movement I now feel is well enough taken care of between the Group One assignments, "Stream-of-Consciousness" writing, and this Group Two, featuring vocal speech. By making here an order of dialogue to monologue, I am not contradicting the recurring movement from inner speech to outer speech but, rather, acknowledging that people first learn to speak through vocal exchange and that soloing comes later followed by the splitting off of inner speech from outer. Solo speech and inner speech occur before school, but putting this development into writing can occur only later and in stages. Play prattle is easy, but holding forth for an audience is hard, and consciously recording and composing inner speech even harder. *As writing assignments*, dialogue should precede monologue, but because inner and outer speech, dialogue and monologue, feed constantly into each other, it is possible to make a case for either progression.

This ambiguity typifies the problem of sequence and explains why any simple linear representation cannot be justified. The source of the ambiguity is that key progressions *recur* in the course of long-range growth, but they recur at another level in another form, creating more dimensions than are dreamt of in scope-and-sequence charts, and that efforts to schematize on paper do not render well. Some of this growth is only thought, some is spoken, and some is written. Carrying a discussion inward as reflection and then writing down one's thoughts about it recapitulates the first pre-school shunting of some speech inward which becomes the prototype for a recurring or cyclic process. By the time she enters school, a child is producing inner speech, but she may not be able to write it down until late elementary school or to *invent* an interior monologue as an oral improvisation until even later, or, to add a further difficulty for perhaps still later, invent an interior monologue in writing. Similarly, a thirdgrader may be able to converse intellectually about some subjects but not be able to sustain more complex thoughts alone—or to tap and organize her solitary thoughts as a written monologue, a whole essay. Perhaps these examples—or, better still, the readers' own—will make clear why a book such as this may serve better as a think-piece for the teacher to use in guiding students individually than in trying to shepherd a whole class at once through the same order of activities.

The particular progression from "Duologue" to "Exterior Monologue" to "Interior Monologue" to "One-Act Play" is one series of assignments that I would not hesitate to recommend as a writing order, because it goes from easy to difficult for most any writer and it has benefited from much experimentation. This is not obligatory, however, since many students could also break into the middle without harm. What may be more nearly obligatory is to do these orally before doing them in writing, because that is almost certain to make written results more *successful*.

We are dealing with two modes here—one of actual speech (transcripts) and one of invented speech (scripts). Transcribing is not composing, but it gives valuable practice in rendering voice on paper and usually involves editing and summarizing. It helps bridge oral speech and written composition. Scripting represents a rather sophisticated kind of composition, of course, since the writer is *simulating* real speech, making up all the roles, and making a statement *by means of* her characters. So this group is strong on the fiction of the theater, drama, and will facilitate the study of dramatic literature. This group leaves us theoretically where *Narrative into Essay* begins—in discourse that is all monological—but in practice students write in both groups concurrently.

We begin with brief suggestions for the easier activities of taking down and shaping actual speech.

Oral Literature

Write down any tale, joke, saying, jingle, verse, or song that you have heard by word of mouth. Make a collection by asking other people for theirs—not just classmates but older people, people from different backgrounds. Make a booklet mixing types, or a booklet on each type such as yarns or sayings or jokes. Leave blank pages for others to add theirs. Pass around. Print up. Give copies to contributors.

Survey

Ask a number of people the same question or questions about something you want to know their view of, then summarize what they said or what you learned. Write up. You might depict results in a graph. First, think out your questions carefully according to what you want to find out and who you think it would be best to ask. When writing up, think of who you want to read these results. Post up, send to someone, or include in a class or local newspaper.

Interview

Choose someone available who is interesting for who they are, what they can do, or special knowledge they have. Think of some questions to ask them but be prepared to make up questions along the way as you hear answers to your first ones. Tape and transcribe and edit later, or take notes and write up later. In either case, summarize with occasional quotes, and think of who else might be interested in knowing what this person said and of how you might best get it to them. (Summarizing a survey or interview develops skill in doing résumés.) "Guitar String"° and "The Camera Looking"° from *The New Yorker* are based respectively on an interview and an interview/visit.

Transcribing Discussion

Discuss in a group of three to five people some topic from local events, your reading, your writing, or the real life of one of you. It could be a problem to solve, a controversy, an interesting idea or insight, or some issue that everyone wants to explore. Tape the discussion and transcribe it together later. You can delete or add or alter lines. Print up or post as is or ask others to read it aloud as a script before an audience that discusses your ideas afterwards. Or write together a summary of your discussion that keeps all the main points and reads smoothly. Print or post this or let one of you deliver it as a talk. This can all be done for a panel discussion too, where each member represents a position or group of other people.

Transcribing Improvisation

Agree as a small group on a main situation or story idea to improvise from and decide who will play which role. Get off by yourselves without others watching, agree on a time and place for the action, establish the real or imagined presence of necessary props, then start a scene. Make up the dialogue and details of action as you go along by paying close attention both to what other players do and to what reactions are prompted within you. What are you and each of the others trying to do in the scene? What are your relationships to each other?

You can stop any time, talk about what happened and how you might want to do it differently, then start in again and make some of these changes. In other words, you can revise your composition of a scene until it seems best to you. Play with factors. What difference would it make if the time or place or some other condition were changed, including who is present at the same time? You can also recast sometimes who is playing which role, or even reverse roles. One technique is to let an extra person side-coach by feeding in observations and suggestions and stimuli that the actors heed without breaking the action.

Leave a tape recorder running while playing and make a "take" of the version of the skit you like best. Transcribe the tape together to make a script to have other people act out or to perform yourselves. You might also print the script in a play booklet with other scripts. Look at the format of printed plays to see how names of speakers and stage directions are put in. Check spellings with others or the dictionary, and test the punctuation by having others read the script aloud to hear if they read it as you mean it.

Duologue

Invent or reproduce a conversation between two people by writing down just what each speaker says in turn. Before each speech set the character's name, followed by a colon. Do not use quotation marks for these speeches. Indicate action and setting by stage directions placed between parentheses. The time, place, and circumstances should be clear from what they say. (800 to 1000 words.) This will be given to others to act out and may also be included in a booklet of plays. Aim for a playing time of 4-5 minutes.

For best results, this assignment should definitely come after a student has improvised duologues with a partner, following more or less the procedure recommended in Transcribing Improvisation. Then improvising alone on paper will seem easy and understandable, and the dynamics of interplay learned through oral improvisation will make scripts more successful sooner, obviating too much disappointing reaction from audiences or those trying to play the scripts. Mostly, however, these scripts really interest others even when not terribly dramatic, partly because performing writing itself enlivens composition for all concerned. This is a very popular assignment.

An easy version of "Duologue" for younger children might go like this:

COMICS

Cut out comic strips and blank out dialogue. Exchange with partners and make up new dialogue. Post. Perhaps copy strip before dialogue is blanked so old and new can be compared. Post both. Draw your own comic strip and write dialogue in balloons.

A very interesting variant of this assignment is to eliminate stage directions and the usual script format and write down only what the characters say, making each speech a new paragraph and perhaps not even naming the characters on the page. Conveying everything entirely through the speeches of the characters leaves more for the reader to infer and will prepare the writer well for invented monologues, but it requires more artful writing and can cause the less accomplished writer to falsify the dialogue in order to get across certain information. Another variant consists of simply increasing the number of characters to three or four. The very different dynamics of a trio (or quartet) are more readily grasped and appreciated after a student has worked with only two. (Again, it's better if oral improvising with three and four precedes writing alone a script with those dynamics.) The only reason for stipulating two is to keep the first experience simple and to establish a base for moving either up in number or down to monologues, which take off best from a two-person drama.

The subject matter of a dialogue is wide open and could take a turn in any of several directions—narrative, if the speakers are recalling events together; essay, if the exchange focuses on fairly impersonal ideas and generalities; drama, if the conversation is an interplay of personalities. The range of the duologue should become apparent when scripts are performed for the whole class. The class might describe for themselves what the differences are among different duologues.

One point of the assignment is certainly to develop the ear. Another is to develop punctuation, which should be explained to the student as a set of signals enabling the reader to reproduce as exactly as possible the original voice. Give examples of intonation, stress, and juncture by putting phrases or sentences on the blackboard that can be read aloud in different ways, and show how punctuation can indicate these things that are otherwise lost on the page. If they learn to punctuate dialogue well, they should have little trouble with other kinds of writing. Show how nearly every fall of intonation calls for some kind of punctuation; which kind may depend on the length of the pause accompanying it. Compare commas, dashes, semicolons, colons, and periods to rest marks in music, which also indicate varying duration. Explain underlining stressed words and other devices for reproducing speech. See pages 231–36 of *Student-Centered Language Arts K-12* for the full development of this approach to punctuation. Both transcribing and scripting offer excellent ways to learn punctuation through vocal intonation, a method that succeeds far better than conventional drills and rules. Dialogue writing also forces students to deal with more kinds of punctuation than are usually taught through grammatical rules (which youngsters get all mixed up).

A final use of duologue can be as a pre-composition writing like those of Group One to loosen a student up and help her produce a lot of ideas to choose from later. For this, one thinks up and names two speakers and gets them going and keeps them going as long as possible, in marathon manner, starting anywhere and going anywhere. The main thing is to use this exchange as a way of getting a lot of ideas down and to surprise one's creativity. The duologue does not have to have form or ending; we just want to see where it goes and what it turns up. For some people this can be an extraordinary experience. Strange and wonderful things come out, along with drivel. Mostly, it's an effective way to draw out material. Then the writer looks it over and plucks out segments to use as they are or simply takes an idea or two and writes about that, maybe even in another form.

Workshop Issues

Doing a reading of a script is the best way to see how to improve it. A couple of the workshop members other than the author can sight-read through it cold. This gives the author a chance to hear misreadings due to bad punctuation or misleading emphasis of sentence structure or word choice. Then they can all talk about the main effect that comes across, getting the viewpoint of both onlookers and readers. (If there are no more than three in the workshop, others might be drafted to read or watch.) Do the characters sound alike or different (an issue of style, we note)? Do they sound like the kind of person they are supposed to be? Or, from what they say and the way they say it, what kind of people are they? Does one dominate—bully or press the other one, initiate the topics? Describe what is happening between the speakers as they talk. Are they getting acquainted, plotting, scrapping, reassuring each other, avoiding something, reminiscing, pleading, etc.?

Where are they and what has brought them together? Have they known each other long? What is their relationship? Ask someone to draw two arrows on the board that represent their relationship—such as two arrows meeting head on, one pursuing the other, etc. Does the conversation have an end? If so, what brings on the end? Is it a slice or fragment?

To bring out a general principle of drama, student attention should bear repeatedly on how close the interaction is between speakers, how well motivated their speeches are, and how much they create effects in each other. Are they really listening and reacting to each other, or are they talking somewhat independently? (You might read to a secondary class Piaget's description of "collective monologue" in children, from *Language and Thought of the Child.)*

Collateral Reading

The students' own scripts will provide some of the handiest and most approachable reading, but, of course, many of these should be performed for the class too. Try to find short two-person playlets appropriate for your students. "Hello Out There" is essentially a two-person play. They are rather rare, but many scenes from plays are splendid duologues, from Greek drama and Shakespeare to modern and juvenile plays. These can be excerpted and done in class as rehearsed readings in the manner of Readers Theater. Some whole short plays like Edward Albee's "The Zoo Story" are duologues. Ballads like "Get Up and Bar the Door" are sometimes a duologue, as are ballad-like poems like Kipling's "Danny Deever." A surprising number of poems are duologues, like William Butler Yeats' light exchange "For Ann Gregory," and J. P. Clark's "Streamside Exchange." Dudley Randall's "Booker T. and W. E. B." is a satire. Many comic strips are duologues, of course. For a duologue short story, see Dorothy Parker's "Telephone Conversation." See also "Dialogue of Ideas."

Exterior Monologue

Make up a character whose way of speaking you feel confident you can imitate; imagine her telling something to another person face to face; then write down exactly what she says and nothing more. The location of the speaker, the identity of her listener, if any, should come through what the speaker says. (800 to 1000 words.) To be performed in a playing time of 3–5 minutes.

This is the more challenging version of the assignment. If you feel it might be too difficult for your students to convey everything through the monologue itself, you can let them add stage directions to establish time, place, and visible circumstances. But students who have been improvising duologues can improvise exterior monologues orally before writing them. Whoever the monologuist is addressing should be physically present during an improvisation and should react continually to what the monologuist says (and nonverbally, of course). This is a very interesting acting assignment, by the way, and improvisers should reverse roles for the same material. There's nothing wrong with the monologuist addressing more than one person if the situation really demands it. What this assignment produces is often called "dramatic monologue" in literary discussion and constitutes not only an important component of plays but also a vehicle for many poems and some short stories and sections of novels. It takes a speaker at the moment of soloing out of dialogue, the moment being afforded by some reason the speaker has to take over and hold forth while the other party holds silent. This stance of the monologuist is the essential stance of the writer.

Workshop Issues

Practical tryouts remain for all scripts the best entrance into discussion and revision. Partners attempting to act out these monologues may not know how physically to place themselves, or how to render the lines if the situation, relationship, or motivation isn't clearly implied. Sometimes a reader gets a good idea for changes in the lines as she feels out the character and the drama of her role. Questions are: Are the time, place, and circumstances of the speaker clear, or important? Do we get an idea of who her listener is and why she is saying this to him? Would she say the same thing to *anyone*, do you think? With a little guidance, students can probably develop the same criteria for judging these papers that the teacher would apply. Does the monologue sound believable as what someone would *speak*? On the other hand, is point or purpose sacrificed to a dull realism? What does the author try to bring out in the monologue—self-revelation of the speaker, something about her relationship with her listener, or something that doesn't have much to do with either?

The scripts will probably scale between strong drama and a kind of essay in which ideas dominate for their own sake. If the character of the speaker is important and she has definite motives in saying what she does to a listener whom she has chosen and with whom she has a relationship, then the results should be dramatic. If any number of different people might be uttering the monologue, and any number of people might be listening, the result almost certainly will be undramatic but may have value as a kind of exposition. (Many students will find writing about ideas easier if they can imagine that someone is saying them to some kind of vague confidant.) Comparing the papers should help bring out what is essentially dramatic and what is something else. A tendency among some students will be to use both interior and exterior monologue as a way of narrating an external story of action—by having the speaker think or speak too much about what is going on right around her. Such papers can be exploited to show what it is that these monologues can do that other forms of writing cannot, and to show what kinds of things are best left to external narrative and description.

Collateral Reading

Once a student has written an exterior monologue or two she should find the reading of poems and stories written in this form much easier to understand, not to mention the many dramatic monologues in the theatre. Young people naturally assume that the voice they hear in something they read is the author's and is utterly reliable and authoritative, whereas actually the voice one hears very frequently in literature is that of a created character speaking in a personal way for personal reasons and under the influence of a listener and certain circumstances. Also, reading and writing dramatic monologue attunes the student to tone, style, and attitude of a tangible speaker so that when the speaker becomes a writer and more anonymous, with attitude and rhetoric more hidden, the student will not become deaf to these key features in writing.

When students are reading a play, you might call attention to the more or less "set" monologues—pieces of "exposition," the Greek messenger's report, long confidences or self-revelations, the long "speech" in Shakespeare that has a unity of its own. We hope the student would come to understand that plays are comprised of soliloquies, monologues, duologues, and dialogues—all of which she will have had a chance to write and which, as practitioner, she will understand better when she reads or hears. As for stage directions, they are a kind of sensory monologue by someone witnessing the action.

August Strindberg's "The Stronger" is a short play that consists entirely of a dramatic monologue, but again such an example is rare. A large number of poems indeed are dramatic monologues. Browning's "My Last Duchess" and "Andrea Del Sarto" and "Fra Lippo Lippi" are pure examples, along with Langston Hughes's "Mother to Son" and John Donne's "The Flea." Some monologuists in poems are types and speak in dialect: John Suckling's "A Ballad Upon a Wedding," Paul Laurence Dunbar's "The Party," Thomas Hardy's "The Man He Killed," and Rudyard Kipling's "Sestina of the Royal Troop." Other monologuists are historical or mythical personages. Three poems interesting to take together are "The Carpenter's Son" by A. E. Housman (uttered by Christ), "The Ballad of the Goodly Fere" by Ezra Pound (spoken by Simon of Zelotes), and "The Journey of the Magi" by T. S. Eliot (spoken by one of the three wise men). Tennyson's "Ulysses" may be taken as either exterior or interior monologue. The time and place of many such poems are left out, but the speaker is definitely a character, and often the person being addressed is indicated, as in the following love poems: John Suckling's "Why So Pale and Wan?," Donne's "Break of Day" and "The Good Morrow," Matthew Arnold's "Dover Beach," and Andrew Marvell's "To His Coy Mistress."

Have students perform or witness performances of poems like these; they will find them much easier to understand than by reading them cold off the page alone. Writing monologues will attune them to invented voices, literary personas. This is true of some short stories too: Ring Lardner's "Zone of Quiet" and "Haircut," George Milburn's "The

Apostate," John O'Hara's "Straight Pool," and "Salute a Thorough-bred," Katherine Mansfield's "The Lady's Maid,"* Sinclair Lewis's "Travel Is So Broadening,"* and Thomas Wolfe's "Only the Dead Know Brooklyn."

Interior Monologue

Make up a character whose way of thinking and speaking you feel confident you can imitate; imagine her somewhere, doing something; then write down in her words what she is thinking and feeling during this situation. Other people may or may not be present. (800 to 1000 words.) To be performed in a playing time of 3–5 minutes.

It may help to explain that this assignment is like "Stream of Consciousness" except that it is fictive instead of actual. If the character is really the student herself, she has the psychological safeguard that others will take it as "invented"; if she attempts to imagine someone else's thoughts and feelings, she gets excellent practice in getting out of her own perspective. In either case, most students will try to give the monologue a "point," try to show something, tell a story, or even editorialize. This assignment allows the student to use vernacular, impromptu speech, for the sake of realism, but invites her to *fashion* something with it. Style is paramount, because the very way of uttering herself characterizes the speaker.

Begin with oral improvisation. A pair off by themselves can define the situation and the characters, then take turns making up a monologue. These might be taped and played back for discussion. The actors should know physically where they are, why they are where they are, and what they are doing while thinking these thoughts. They utter the thoughts aloud in the tradition of the stage soliloquy. A transcribed improvisation might, in fact, be edited and revised to fulfill this assignment. On the other hand, someone who has done such oral improvisation may well be able to go right to paper.

In some junior high classes experimenting with these script-writing assignments, ninth-graders performed their scripts before eighth-graders and seventh-graders. Besides affording the authors a very interested audience outside their own class, the younger students picked up from the performance what the assignments were meant to produce. Such illustration and example make assignments very clear and inspire other students to try their hand at them.

Like the rest of the dramatic writing in this series, interior monologue may be written as a poem or short story, in which case stage directions would be omitted. If stage directions are included, that should mean that the paper is intended as a script for others to play. The need to self-characterize through the style of speaking naturally suggests doing this assignment as a poem, because the language becomes so important.

In working with their own and literary interior monologue, students should become aware of the occasional splitting of the voice when the speaker changes tone and attitude and almost begins to sound like another person. When she asks questions and gives commands, who is she speaking to? Only herself. But one part of her is speaking to another, and sometimes the other part answers. In other words, most interior monologues are dialogues between different inner selves. To some extent, actual dialogues may be regarded as externalized inner speech; or perhaps we should regard inner speech as dialogues that one has or has had with other real people. In any case, self-division, as signaled by changes of voice and attitude and by questions, commands, threats, etc., should be noted because of its great importance for the inner conflict that makes up so much of literature and life.

One way of showing interpretation of a play or novel is for students to make up an interior monologue for a certain character at a certain moment in the action; how the student characterizes the speaker, what language and which thoughts she attributes to her, and the way she works the monologue into the story should all reveal the extent of her understanding. This is an example of how an activity worthwhile for its own sake may also, secondarily, help the teacher to assess comprehension. Evaluation should always follow this principle of being part of an authentic learning task.

Like the other assignments in this group, this one should help students to *listen*, to hear the way other people speak, to get an ear for authentic character as it comes solely through a voice. The creation of a real voice with a definite personality behind it, having its own tone and style, is an important part of all writing, from drama to essay. Also, interior and exterior monologues require discriminating between talking to oneself and talking to another. Some of these papers will undoubtedly sound as if they are spoken to another person; in some good way this should be pointed out. And some papers will probably present a character speaking in a vacuum, dissociated from her surroundings, not doing anything but just thinking in a generalized way; although this too should be pointed out, and does violate the assignment, still it may be an easier entrée into idea writing for many students than trying right off to do an essay. Once again, describing is better than judging.

Workshop Issues

Do trial readings and revise according to results. Can you tell where the character is and what she's doing? Can you tell what the speaker is like? Does the monologue sound believable as *thoughts*, especially for that character? Perhaps she thinks things merely for the benefit of the reader, or explains things to herself that she already knows. Perhaps her words are too well chosen or too "big," her sentences too well constructed. Can you tell what the real author was trying to do —reveal character, tell a story from the inside, get across a satiric point?

Collateral Reading

Literary counterparts are soliloquies from plays, certain poems, and some short stories and sections of novels. Modern musicals often include songs that are soliloquies, like "If I Were a Rich Man" from *Fiddler on the Roof*. Some poems are Amy Lowell's "Patterns," Browning's "Soliloquy of the Spanish Cloister" and "The Laboratory," Keats' "Ode to a Nightingale," and T. S. Eliot's "Gerontion" and "Love Song of J. Alfred Prufrock." A lot of poems are modified interior monologues and are more accessible when approached this way. Comparing these literary soliloquies with their own should bring out quickly to students how stylized and "unrealistic" the literary ones are: the needs of the stage, of prosody, and of narrative necessitate this. Eugene O'Neill's *The Emperor Jones* is virtually a sustained interior monologue put on stage. Among short stories are Dorothy Parker's "But the One on the Right"* and Katherine Mansfield's "Late at Night." Most of James Joyce's *Ulysses* and sections of other novels consist of interior monologue.

One-Act Play

Imagining characters and events like the kind of people and events you have had a chance to observe in real life, and using the form of dialogue and stage directions of a standard script, write a play that would take twenty to thirty minutes to perform and that could actually be performed. What you want to show, or what you want to do to the audience, is up to you.

Students can estimate together how long this piece should be; relating playing time to script length is educational in itself. Previous dramatic efforts and professional plays can be used as a measure.

The stipulation about realism of characters and events is designed to preclude the common imitations of movies and television and science fiction and also to keep scripts playable. Although students usually see their wild situations and sensational events as products of their own "imagination," this is seldom so; they unconsciously rehash hundreds of old stories. Fantasies of real value are original distortions of commonly accepted reality, and true imagination consists in seeing the familiar in a new way. At some time the assignment can certainly be to do a fantasy play, but the craft of staging can be better worked out first with relatively realistic action.

A variation of this assignment is to write the play as a script for television or the movies. Get a sample script of a television play or film and let the students see the format of it and learn the technical terms required for camera angles and movements. Differences among the media can be brought out by discussing the possibilities that open or close when the viewer and the set are fixed and when the viewer (camera) is mobile and selective. Ideally, of course, a film or videotape would be made from the scripts. In all cases, the different kinds of acting entailed—when on stage before a live audience or close-up before a camera—should be discussed as the different scripts are read or produced. The essential thing with this variation is to develop a sense of how the writer adapts to her medium, an important practical fact that may be related to Shakespeare's writing for the peculiarities of the Elizabethan stage.

Workshop Issues

The kind of questions—technical, psychological, and literary—that are appropriate for discussing professional plays are appropriate for the student offerings. What is happening among the people? What does this lead to? Are soliloquies, monologues, duologues, and stage directions (sensory monologues) used for what they can do best—appropriately? (This assignment is, after all, a culmination of their work with these four kinds of discourse.) Performance, or even just the attitude of performance, can bring out a lot of technical strengths and weaknesses concerning such theater problems as: too many characters on stage with nothing to do, speeches that are too long, confusing transitions in action or dialogue, action inadequately prepared for, individual lines and passages of dialogue that cannot be spoken with any truth or beauty, etc. If the action is continuous in one time and place, why did the author choose *that* time and place? If the action is broken into scenes occurring at different times and places, did the author choose them best for what she seems to be trying to do, or could some of the scenes be deleted, perhaps in favor of dramatizing some off-stage action that we are only told about? How is the problem of "exposition" handled, of getting background or off-stage information across to the audience in a plausible way? Of course, it is not necessary to ask such questions arbitrarily; they merely represent the kinds of issues you can help call attention to, if you exploit the spontaneous comments of the students about each other's plays.

Collateral Reading

One major purpose of this assignment is to put the student in the role of the professional not only for self-expression but so that as play reader and audience she can spontaneously understand what the professional is doing, without the necessity of the teacher explaining plays to her or spoiling the pleasure and impact of plays by tedious analysis. Having done a play puts the student on the inside of the whole game of drama, so that not only is comprehension facilitated, but the student becomes much more involved in the ways and ends of plays in general. The reading and performing of the plays that come from this assignment should be interwoven with the reading or performing of professional one-act plays, some of which might also be available on tape or disc.

The writing of plays can be correlated with literature other than drama. A valuable and interesting assignment, in lieu of testing students about a short story, real narrative, or narrative poem, is to ask them to convert the story to a short play, or to consider the feasibility of doing so. How easy would it be? What would be the difficulties? What changes would you *have* to make? With what gains and losses? The differences between narrative—a report of what happened—and drama—a presentation of what is happening—should become clear. Which of their own plays might have been better done as a narrative? Again, in lieu of traditional testing by factual questions or essay questions, ask the students to dramatize a scene from a play they are reading that took place off-stage and was merely reported; or to do the same with a scene from a novel that the narrator only referred to. Such assignments ask that the student extrapolate what she has seen of characters in other parts of the play or novel, and that she understand the point of the off-stage scene and the overall action into which it fits. Students who are not ready to write abstractly about what they understand of their reading may nevertheless understand well and can show their degree of comprehension in this mode.

Dialogue of Ideas

Let two voices, A and B, discuss or argue some controversial issue. Set this down in duologue form without stage directions. Make up this dialogue straight off for about thirty minutes. This can be performed by others, printed up, or used as a basis for further writing.

The main purpose of this is to produce as many ideas about the subject as possible, to explore all sides of an issue without feeling compelled to build up a single case that avoids contradictions. The issue might come from anywhere—group discussion, current local issues, other writing (see "Proverb and Saying"), or reading. Many students who go blank before "Discuss the following . . ." or who will attempt to guess what the teacher wants to hear about a certain book may come up with better and more honest ideas by this approach. The very process of question-answer, parry-thrust, statement-response is inherently dramatic and hence more appealing to some students than exposition as a way of getting into explicit statements of generalization. Also, as another approach to exposition and argumentation, this assignment has the advantage of forcing the student to consider different sides of an issue; it may break down dogmatism and the simple, settled point of view. In essay writing students often feel that they are supposed to build up a one-sided case and overwhelm the reader with it; for the sake of this, and in dread of having their argument torn apart later, they sacrifice depth, range, complexity, and discrimination.

Naming characters *A* and *B* aims to disembody the dialogue and slant it more easily toward ideas, but some students might work better with less abstract designations like Mother and Daughter or with imaginative names like Colonel Beauregard and Hard-Hearted Hannah. This ties in with role-playing.

The absence of stage directions emphasizes a topic by reducing setting and action, as in the following student example.

SHOULD DRIVING AGE BE RAISED?

ADULTS: **The driving age should be raised to around 18.**
TEENAGERS: **Why what good would it do?**
ADULTS: **It would decrease the number of accidents.**
TEENAGERS: **It wouldn't make that much difference because most accidents occur with kids 18 and 21.**

ADULTS: **That may be true but there are still a lot of accidents that could be avoided with kids 16–17.**

TEENAGERS: **In that case raise the age to 21 or 25 and stop almost all accidents.**

ADULTS: **Now that's going too far.**

TEENAGERS: **It's about as ridiculous as raising it to 18. Besides it's easy for you to say because you're over 18 and you've got your license. But you wouldn't say it if you were 16 or 17.**

ADULTS: **That isn't the reason, it's just that teenagers lack experience.**

TEENAGERS: **Everybody lacks experience just starting out. Even if we don't drive until we're 30 we will still lack experience.**

ADULTS: **Another reason is that teenagers lack pride and respect.**

TEENAGERS: **We have just as much pride as anyone else, and why have respect? We are always being put down, by the way we dress, and things we do, etc.**

ADULTS: **Where is the pride? And the way you dress is bad.**

TEENAGERS: **Kids take better care of their cars than adults. As for the way we dress, why is it bad, because you didn't dress that way? We think the way you dressed when you were kids was stupid too. Just because you didn't do it doesn't mean it's bad or wrong.[1]**

This assignment ties in with the writing of spontaneous trains of thought if we consider that interior monologue is really interior dialogue, that reflecting on some subject is a kind of colloquy born of previous points of view which we have incorporated from contact with others and from changing experiences. Naturally, the richness of this reflection will depend a lot on our openness or imperviousness to others and on the leanness or variety of our experiences. This is why, generally, a lot of class discussion is important: thinking is to some extent an internalization of speech, of conversations one has had and heard. The workshop discussion approach serves this end constantly. Impromptu vocal dialogues on student-chosen topics would do it even more specifically.

[1] A ninth grader at Lexington High School, Lexington, Massachusetts.

One tenth grader put his dialogue, below, into the mouths of two personality types—the idealist and the practicalist. He chose the narrative way of quoting speakers.

I had been watching him writing for five minutes. "What's your idea?" I asked.

"It's about this guy writing an English composition," he replied without altering his activity.

"What do you think you'll get?" I asked laughing.

"Well, it follows the assignment and I know what I'm talking about firsthand—about a "B." There, all finished."

"That's nice; I haven't even started yet," I said wryly.

"The trouble with you is that you want to stun the world with a measly English composition. Your chances of stunning even the teacher are only about fifty-fifty at best. Why risk it? Why not play it safe like me? Why lose?"

"Because it's worth it to lose for that one hope that you might win." It sounded trite, but I felt oddly inspired.

"So what if you 'win.' You get an "A" and that's it."

"You also get the personal satisfaction of knowing you had a good idea and succeeded. Less important but also present is the admiration you get from your friends. The infrequent gain is certainly worth the frequent loss. You also know that at least for a few weeks that composition is going to be remembered as something special and that you were the author of it. Even if it is rejected by your teacher and by your colleagues, if you think you have succeeded, then you have."

"What an idealist," he said disgustedly.

"On the basis just of my attitude towards English compositions, I don't think you can make an accurate conclusion. But I would like to think of myself as some sort of idealist. But everyone is an idealist to some extent."

"Not me," he said casually. "I'm a practicalist."

"If you are what you say you are, you're doomed to oblivion."

"How so?" he asked, more interested.

"Take three examples—past, present, and future—of the idealist and of a 'practicalist.' First, consider the past. I'm certain that you've heard of Miguel de Cervantes, author of *Don Quixote*."

"Yea, look where his idealism got him—in trouble with the Spanish Inquisition for the greater part of his life." He thought he had me.

"You agree then that Cervantes was an idealist."

"Well, yes he had to be to write a book like *Don Quixote*," he said warily.

"Admittedly, Cervantes had a hard life in physical terms, but we're discussing the question of oblivion, and even you are quite familiar with Cervantes."

"But what about scientists?" he said, trying to recover.

"Galileo," I replied quickly. "Take Galileo. Everybody was sure that the sun moved around the earth, so he suggested that it was the other way around and was right. That's idealism for you in that he disregarded practical considerations in pursuance of what seemed an absurdity, and I'm sure that you remember him."

"What was his ideal?"

"I suppose the ideal of every good scientist, the quest for truth. Then take the practical scientist of that age. He did the practical thing and read Aristotle. Everybody 'knew' that Aristotle was right so the guy made it through life pretty easily. But do you ever hear about some guy who did something like that? No."

"But things aren't like that today," he said desperately.

"Alright, take the present. Your claim not to be an idealist will never be remembered. Sure, you can come up with practical ideas for slight betterment of your business that, if you're smart, will improve it through the years. But you're not going to do anything which you will be remembered for because any great ideas or inspirations have to transcend practical considerations. Your problem is that the details will guide your ideas whereas your ideas should guide the details."

"An example?" he said stubbornly.

"The Wright brothers," I replied. "The lightest engine made at the time was much too heavy for any of their aircraft and they couldn't afford one anyway. Notice the results."

"O.K., O.K., what about the future?"

"Say that sometime in the future there should happen to be an atomic war and and there were only a few survivors."

"Ha!" he exclaimed triumphantly, "where would your idealist be then?"

"I agree that alone the full-fledged idealist could not survive. But as long as the others keep him alive, he will base that life on ideals and formulate the beginning of a perfect civilization. When that civilization has reached its peak, it will remember that man as the father of that civilization and will not remember the man who brought him water or food every morning."

"But what is so important about being remembered," he said flustered. "The important thing is to have a happy life while you're alive. Once you're dead, you're dead, and you're not going to know whether you were remembered or not."

"No, the important thing is to die knowing that you have lived for something. Many idealists are not remembered. But they die knowing that they have spent their lives striving for that ideal of whatever their pursuits may be. Whether they reach it or not, they know that in their striving their lives had some purpose and that they were not just vegetables. For the idealist who is not remembered, he knows to himself that his life has had some worthwhile purpose. For the one who is remembered, that world knows that his life has had some worthwhile purpose but the important thing is the individual. Either way he can't lose. Hey, what are you doing?"

"Ripping up my first composition so that I can start a new one. Now to think of a good idea . . ."[2]

This mode of discourse allows the student to present in an entertaining way a dialectic of ideas that may be also an expression of two inner selves in conflict.

Inasmuch as a duologue risks dichotomizing thought, three or four voices would be better, if a student can handle them. Or a third voice can be added after the duologue has gone on a while. A workshop group alert to the danger of crude dualism might suggest that a writer continue her dialogue with a third voice.

Workshop Issues

Although the teacher may warn the student at the outset of some obvious pitfalls, such as letting A and B repeat themselves in a circle, or having a virtual monologue in which B is too stupid or acquiescent to hold up her end, it is probably more useful in the long run to let the students who will, commit these mistakes, especially since this is the

[2] Brooks Academy, North Andover, MA.

kind of assignment that should be done a number of times. Reading papers aloud as scripts and then discussing them should bring out such troublesome qualities of the dialogue, not of course as a rebuke to the author but as a way of describing what she has done. If one student points out that another's dialogue is no dialogue at all, because B is a straight man who only mumbles assent or makes innocuous remarks from time to time, this is the opportunity to help the author understand something that is limiting her thinking: perhaps her preconceptions and prejudices on the subject are so strong that she simply cannot see more than one point of view; or something about that subject threatens her and she does not want to explore it. (Of course, the subject might be poor.) If someone finds a paper repetitious, the author should be encouraged to ask herself why A and B got stuck and started circling at a certain point, or perhaps the group can answer this for her if she can't.

Ask which of the papers had the hottest dispute between A and B, which saw A and B collaborating best, and which kept A and B from coming to grips with each other or the subject. Do A and B merely state ideas or do they try also to prove them (the difference between opinion and persuasion)? Which produced the best ideas, the most interesting discussion of the subject? It may be that sometimes a group will be able to go on and correlate the kind of dynamics that went on with the quality and number of ideas produced. This is a chance to see something of their own real-life discussions. Did A and B contend or collaborate more? Did they pick up directly what the other had just said or did they keep starting new trains of thought? Which kind of dialogue seems to be most productive of ideas and the most interesting? It's important for the teacher not to have too strong a preconception about answers to these questions, or to use the questions as a way of arriving at a formula.

Rewriting of these papers might go two ways. One is pursued in the next assignment, but many dialogues might, with some editing and revision, remain as compositions in their own right, as well perhaps as being redone as an essay. The next assignment is rather difficult, so some students will have to stop at this stage, in which case it would be good for them to revise this assignment here into a finished piece that can be played out as a reading and discussed or printed in a booklet or newspaper. Some might become duologue poems.

Collateral Reading

Inasmuch as this assignment exploits the drama of dialectic as a means to exposition and argumentation, anything the teacher does that strengthens the drama is very much to the point. Tapes, video-tapes, and transcripts of debates, court trials, hearings, and panel discussions would be of enormous help in teaching dialogue and dialectic simultaneously. Many "problem plays," such as some by Shaw and Ibsen, are essentially dialectical, and everyone knows how well the "adversary process" of trials lends itself to theater. Poems such as Samuel Daniels' "Ulysses and the Sirens," Richard Wilbur's "Two Voices in a Meadow," Frost's "West Running Brook," William Blake's "The Clod and the Pebble," Yeats' "Dialogue of Self and Soul," or G. M. Hopkins' "The Leaden Echo and the Golden Echo" would be appropriate for maturer students, but many other poems consist of two or more voices creating character interaction and interplay of ideas. As some of these titles indicate, the points of view can be represented by objects as well as personages.

Dialogue Converted to Essay

Rewrite your Dialogue by merging its two voices into one, but without sacrificing any good ideas. Feel free to add new ideas, get rid of weak ones, change words, and reorganize. You may regard this as a speech, editorial, or essay and follow up accordingly.

As direct conversion of dialogue to monologue, this assignment embodies a crucial, long-range process.

It's important that the topics of these dialogues and their conversions be something that students can naturally be expected to know about —commonalities of experience—and not topics requiring research or special experience. Topics drawn from international affairs or national politics beg the student to repeat opinions and information she has heard and read. It is best for topics to come out of students' own efforts to think through issues they run into or from other work they are doing. Often a group will generate a topic together.

As so often, the teacher's problem is to decide how much to forestall possible discouragement by warning students of pit-falls and how much to let them encounter the difficult issues first through trial and error. Much depends on how heavy the penalties for error are. If a student feels she gets "shot down" in class for bad judgment on a paper, or that the teacher docks her grade a lot or marks the paper harshly, she may feel bitter that she wasn't warned more about what she might do wrong in the assignment. If the penalties are not too severe and the class atmosphere is supportive and collaborative, it's preferable to let students learn about crucial issues by doing first and getting feedback afterward. Ample opportunity for help and revision before final commitment makes the chances of success better than on a one-shot, win-all-lose-all situation.

Workshop Issues

The merging of the two voices entails more than just combining the best ideas of *A* and *B*, for the good ideas of both may contradict each other. It's crucial that the student be helped to solve this problem of dialectic by finding appropriate words such as *but, however, nevertheless, although*, etc., or by reaching up to a higher level of abstraction and finding a concept there that will harmonize the ideas. Some students will be tempted to solve the problem by lopping off one of the ideas even though they know it's good, by placing the ideas so far apart that the contradiction is not obvious, or by invoking some cliché about happy mediums. It must become clear that none of these subterfuges is necessary—that if two opposing ideas are both good, there's always a way to contain them both in one essay if one finds their proper relationship or finds a framing idea big enough to accommodate both. This issue should be a major focus of discussion as papers are read.

If the group remarks that a paper seems too simple or contradictory or platitudinous, the group should feel obligated to help the author, which can be done by reading her original dialogue to see what she might have done. Somebody might say, "Why didn't you leave that in—then your paper wouldn't have been so simple or one-sided?" Or, if the dialogue was itself too simple, or one-sided, it may be pointed out that she could have added new ideas. Or if the consensus is that the paper contradicts itself, the group should be asked how the opposition of ideas could be resolved. If any of the three subterfuges mentioned above are suggested, try to get the group to scrutinize them until the objections to them are recognized and better alternatives proposed. If members agree that both ideas should be kept and also agree that they are contradictory, then we are square in the middle of a paradox—an opposition that only seems to be so because the concept that would harmonize the contrary propositions is left unstated. In addition to getting the group to supply this concept for paper *X*, you might at this point bring in some calculated paradoxes from poems and essays—like Keats' "April shroud"—the whole point of which is to make the reader step back to an unaccustomed perspective and find for herself the missing harmonizer. Seeing joy and sorrow as aspects of the same thing is typical of the process of mind enlargement that converting the dialogue may entail. Or paper X may simply fail to *acknowledge* the opposition by the use of a concessive clause, or to qualify by the use of a proviso or conditional clause. This finding of specialized words for the relationship of ideas is a logical matter, and such problems of logic are better handled as they come up repeatedly in particular instances on student papers than en bloc as a separate subject.

Unless the original dialogue developed the ideas in an unusually orderly way, converting to essay is sure to entail also a problem of organization. Spontaneous conversation is apt to string ideas like beads, without considering which should go first and which later, or to dwell on some ideas too long and not enough on others, or to circle around and pick up ideas the second time for further development. Since our spontaneous thoughts are apt to come out in the same way, revising the dialogue is much like reordering and recasting our original thoughts about something. Appropriate questions about organization might be: Would it make any difference if the order of paragraphs were changed (if read aloud, the reader should signal with her hand at the end of each paragraph)? Did X begin with her main assertions and then develop and illustrate them, or did she work up to the main assertions as the conclusion? Which would be better? (Certainly a relative matter.) Does X talk about the same thing in different places? For a good reason, or just by chance?

If the subject was about something the group had written on in common, it might compare papers as a point of departure for discussing the original topic. If each student wrote on a different subject, comparison of papers should bring out the different problems of the different topics: Was this subject harder to organize than that one? Does this have special pitfalls?

Lastly, these papers can be discussed, treated, and commented on in much the same way as the later expository assignments, in *Narrative into Essay*, that they are supposed to lead up to. Students should be helped to notice and assess the ratio between generality and illustration, the ratio between the amount of explanation and the difficulty of the idea being explained, and the ratio between the maintenance of an initial idea and the introduction of new ideas. As questions: Is the paper too abstract; does it fail to supply enough examples to make the ideas clear and interesting? Is the paper an itemization of concrete things without enough ideas to enable the reader to relate them? Does the author dwell too long on the obvious and take too much for granted with more complicated or controversial ideas? Do ideas come so thick and fast that you can't remember what the main line is? Or is each new idea related in turn to the main idea? These are basic and perennial questions for any reader of any idea piece—at least if she is having any *trouble* reading it. If a student who is bothered by something about a theme she hears gets used to helping the writer diagnose the difficulty, she will naturally begin to place herself more in the reader's position when *she* is writing.

Collateral Reading

The same as for other idea writing found in the latter part of *Narrative into Essay*; many editorials in newspapers and magazines and many speeches, which might be found recorded or printed.

Group Three
NARRATIVE INTO ESSAY

This group of assignments goes from concrete narratives to more distilled ones and thence to the ultimate distillation of narrative—generalization. So the shift is from the past tense to the present tense of generalization—*what happened* to *what happens*. Narrating is monologuing, but it *embeds* or *summarizes* dialogue, that is, incorporates dialogue either verbatim or indirectly. We begin with a kind of throwback to dialogue, two-way correspondence, thence to the monologue of diary and on to other shifts in time-space perspective that array the variety of first- and third-person, first- and secondhand narrative. Then come some assignments coordinating narrative with general statement in ratios that increasingly shift emphasis onto the explicit distilled ideas and away from the sources or documentation of the ideas. These gains and losses are important to explore—the why as well as the how. Narrative becomes exposition by gradual shifts, and this continuous bridging between abstraction levels needs to be followed in some way, sometimes as an order of writing, sometimes merely as a focus of awareness for teacher and students.

This group of assignments, like the last, covers both actuality and fiction. I've tried to treat them together to show correlation but also to separate them because issues of growth and difficulty are different for each. Narrating and generalizing from what happened in actuality entail certain problems of logic and abstraction not encountered in fictionalizing, which has other problems of conceptualizing, namely, selecting and relating personages, actions, and objects so that they all symbolize ideas beyond themselves. Narratives of actuality may make a general statement too, but this usually has to be stated more explicitly, in a sort of separate editorializing, whereas fiction *implies* generalizations through its running metaphors. Fictional narrative *simulates* actual narrative and hence *appears* to be of the same abstraction level, but to the extent that it does not report true events, its composition problems are different. It, too, symbolizes real experience but not directly, and it compresses narrative and essay in one

71

discourse by saying *what happens* while purporting to tell *what happened.* Invented narrative represents greater sophistication because its elements have all been conceived as a perfected, self-sufficient construction. A good reporter, by contrast, has no such choices but must let chips fall where they may. Art lays another dimension onto narrative. (The same is true for drama, since plays merely *simulate* conversation, being calculated to imply *what happens* through *what is happening.*)

All this means that a growth sequence or even an order of difficulty for fiction cannot be assumed to correspond with that of actual narrative. Far from it. Whereas writing a true group story, or chronicle, gleaned from multiple sources calls for more previous composition experience and greater abstractive powers than writing autobiography, the counterpart of chronicle, impersonal third-person fiction, is probably the easiest for a novice (partly because published children's stories and folk tales run more to that type). Telling a fiction as a diary or an exchange of letters, or from any sustained inside point of view, is very sophisticated and not likely to occur to most children until they've seen examples. Aside from the strong influence of conventions in children's literature that may be merely cultural, it's probably true that developmental order in narrative techniques runs just about the reverse of that for actuality. That is, however homely and familiar in real life a narrative method may be—letter or eyewitness report—it becomes very artful indeed when simulated as a fictional device.

I think that to the extent children grow slowly into creating multilevel discourse, such as the kind of double story that an identified narrator creates, then a real biological factor of growth constrains children's own storytelling to good old anonymous, omniscient, uncomplicated narration as in fairy tales. On the other hand, perhaps more early experience hearing and reading stories told in a greater variety of points of view might remove sooner most children's "natural" balking at equivocality and relativism, traits of narrative whereby the teller and the told-about form two levels of storying and raise issues of bias and reliability. The first time I read a story written in the first person (in sixth grade) I was shocked and annoyed. Who was this *I* getting in the way of the story? There was only one *I*, and I was it. But it's very possible that this reaction (of "cognitive dissonance"!) may be prolonged if not induced by the traditional school diet of third-person narratives. Even in secondary school students are seldom introduced to the lower-order or source documents of social studies and history—transcripts, letters, diaries, autobiography, and memoir—where particular voices can be heard and have to be assessed for bias and flavor. Too infrequently during elementary school do children read either in literature or in other subject areas a narrative not written from the anonymous, omniscient point of view. This is right for folk literature, which emphasizes a primal universality, but textbooks of literature and other discourse use this narrative mode for other reasons, mainly to assert an impartiality that is not real and to influence children, wrongly, to conform to a standardized reality. I am thinking first of books written especially for textbook publishers but also of many overly conventional anthologies used in school.

A sequence for writing, should it exist, would not necessarily coincide with a sequence for reading or oral discourse. And yet people learn better, I think, if speaking, reading, listening, and writing are closely interwoven. As I've just suggested, for one thing, how early youngsters acquire the full repertory of narrative techniques for their writing may depend a lot on the reading material they have been exposed to. So in describing writing assignments I've tried to relate them to kinds of reading matter that could be read in conjunction with them. In the case of the assignments covered in this group, this opens up the vast array of old and modern fiction and of nonfiction narratives and articles and essays running all across the curriculum through the physical and social sciences and philosophy. Poetry runs virtually the whole spectrum; students could do most of these assignments not only as fiction but as poems.

Interwoven here with the more fully developed assignments are briefly indicated assignments that I've added to fill in needed areas and to provide some easier activities for less developed students. Some are just as important as those dealt with in more detail, but in the context of the whole presented here do not seem to need as much elaboration. Thus we begin this group with imaginative kinds of storytelling (good for any age) that should always be in the narrative repertory.

Story Starters

Get an unfinished sentence or opening from the teacher or someone else and take it from there to invent the rest. "Just as Henrietta glanced up the block to see if the bus was coming she noticed with a sudden fear a familiar figure turn into a nearby shop. . . ."

Being Something Else

Imagine you are an object and make up a story told from that object's point of view about some predicament or typical situation it is in. (How about a kitchen blender or a flower vase?) Do the same thing for an animal or plant. Try to feel and talk as it would. You might agree with partners to write as the same object or animal and compare afterwards and post together or make into a booklet.

Photo Stories

Cut out several photos from magazines and bring to class to make up stories about. Spread out and exchange with those of partners. Some might show still scenes, some people in action, some people talking, some a person alone, some a place, and so on so that you and partners have a choice of different kinds of stories, dialogues, monologues, or mood pieces. Your story can be a poem. Write what the picture you have chosen seems to say to you about what is going on or what the circumstances are. If an essay comes to mind instead of a story, write that. Post compositions and pictures side by side to make a classroom exhibit, then make into a booklet to pass around. Perform dialogues and monologues with the picture in view.

Cut out or photograph eight or ten pictures among which some objects, people, and places recur from time to time so that a group can make up stories from a given or random order. Change the order, change the story. Compare stories for the same series. Tell or write. Or tell first, write later. Post series of pictures with story running below or alongside. Print booklet of stories, including pictures.

Dreams

Jot down a dream soon afterwards so you'll remember it better, or keep a notebook of dreams regularly. Tell the dream to a partner or group until you have it well in mind, listen to what they have to say about it, then write it as a story. If it didn't end, or ended in a way you don't like, add an ending or change the original one. Read it to a group and talk about whether others have similar dreams. Or rehearse and record your story for others to listen to. Or include in a booklet of other stories by you or classmates.

Tall Tales

Make up an outlandish yarn by telling something you or someone else is supposed to have done. Make it close enough to possibility to intrigue the reader, but exaggerate so much that it humorously puts him on too. Tall tales are like boasts or wild claims but done for fun. Some could take off from each other in the spirit of "top this."

Correspondence

Invent a series of letters between two people. Date the letters and have each correspondent write at least twice.

Correspondence is dialogue at a distance; that is the connection between this assignment and the previous work with duologues and plays, which imitate face-to-face discourse. In making up a series of letters, the student is in effect imitating the way people talk to each other when they do not see each other, cannot get immediate feedback, and are not under the influence of each other's presence, even though they are known to each other and have some relationship.

This assignment can be done at very different levels of maturity. Younger students will probably use it as a way of telling and saying things to someone they know well, thus reproducing or reflecting actual correspondence they have had or would like to have. One would not expect such correspondences to have much point or art. Older students, who could read epistolary fiction during the assignment, might well use the assignment as a way of telling and dramatizing a story calculated to reveal character or situation. And, of course, younger children ought to have plenty of occasions to write single letters in school to various parties before doing this assignment—to relatives, pen pals, places they want information, and so on. Help them set up a place to send and receive advice letters—a class box or newspaper column—and make writing, reading, and discussing advice letters a strong, continuous activity.

Each letter is a kind of monologue, as the whole correspondence is a kind of dialogue. And like those discourses, letters may take many directions, deal with very different subjects. They may report recent events (narrative) or exchange ideas and specific information (exposition) or consist of questions, admonitions, commands, pleas, threats, etc. (drama). They may range from tight interplay of personalities to impersonal intellectualizing. The reading and discussing of the papers should bring out all these differences as a matter of descriptive recognition.

Workshop Issues

This assignment facilitates discussing style. Do the two correspondents sound alike or can you tell them apart if you read scattered excerpts? Are there differences in their vocabulary, the kinds of sentences they use, or the way they move from topic to topic? Can you say what each is like as a person? The fact that the correspondence is colloquial writing does not mean authors should not be responsible for spelling, punctuation, and other mechanics. Responders should consider the possibility that mistakes are intentional in characterizing certain kinds of correspondents, but, on the other hand, they may often have occasion to remark that such-and-such a well-to-do or well-educated person, as characterized in X's letters, would know better than to commit such-and-such a mistake, or would not use the kind of kiddish expression or slang that X has attributed to him. Students speaking a nonstandard dialect may adopt standard dialect without losing face in order to render a character authentically, since realism of style calls for such role-playing. A key question is whether workshop members can tell that the two correspondents are really writing, not speaking aloud. How can they tell?

Discussion of both professional stories and student themes could turn on a few key questions: What is going on between the correspondents? (Led up to by asking why they are not together and why they are writing to each other.) Does the correspondence only show character, does it piece together reports of action, or does it mainly just stake out a situation? Is there a climax? The motive for writing the letters should become clear during discussion.

Collateral Reading

With older students, the writing of this assignment might be preceded by the reading of a story or two that are written entirely as letters. Many students, however, are so prone to imitating content that it might be better to read such stories afterwards. In any case, doing the assignment should enhance comprehension and appreciation of epistolary fiction and actual correspondence.

In most libraries, letters are placed near or in autobiography. Whatever a student's interests, some correspondence exists related to it, because letters of people in all fields have been published. See Columbus's letters to Queen Isabella, Van Gogh's letters to his brother (*Dear Theo*), Bernard Shaw's and Ellen Terry's correspondence, George Jackson's letters from prison, and Laura Ingalls Wilder's *West From Home*. For excerpted single letters and both one-way and two-way correspondence see the "Interaction" section of *Points of Departure*. Advice-column letters of the Dear Abby sort appear all the time in newspapers and magazines and are very popular with youngsters, especially as many feature subjects like sports or health or boy-girl relations.

Epistolary fiction flourished in the eighteenth century especially: Samuel Richardson's *Clarissa Harlowe* and *Pamela*, Tobias Smollet's *Humphrey Clinker*, Pierre Choderlos de la Clos' *Dangerous Liaisons*, and Fanny Burney's *Evelina*. But prior reading in modern fiction might include Mark Harris's *Wake Up, Stupid*, Alice Walker's *The Color Purple*, John P. Marquand's *The Late George Apley*, J. D. Salinger's "Hapworth 16, 1924," and short stories like Ambrose Bierce's "Jupiter Doke, Brigadier General,"* Henry James' "A Bundle of Letters"* Thomas Bailey Aldrich's "Marjorie Daw," Roger Angell's "The Floto Letters," and John Updike's "Dear Alexandros." Poems in letter form include Kenneth Rexroth's "A Bread and Butter Letter," Archibald MacLeish's "Epistle to the Left in the Earth," Louise Bogan's "A Letter," Karl Shapiro's "V Letter," and Robert Bly's "A Missouri Traveller Writes Home, 1846."

Diary

Keep a diary for about five weeks, making about five entries in the diary per week. Allow ten to fifteen minutes to write each entry; write down whatever seems important to you on that day. You will have a choice of what to show of it to others. It will be used as the basis for later writing.

A great many things can be done with this assignment. It has several purposes: to help make writing habitual and natural; to give importance to everyday occurrences and feelings; to encourage the notation of specific things of the moment; to tie writing to firsthand experiences; to create a record of enough duration to provide time perspective on events; and to produce a lot of original material for later writing.

Diaries come naturally to young people, especially during adolescence. Writing one is perhaps like confiding. For this reason it may be important to assure the student that he will have a chance to select what he will present to public view. Many students who traditionally don't like to write English themes can get quite interested in keeping a diary and will write an enormous amount, more than they ever would for class—and more than the teacher could ever read. Even though these entries will not be directly subject to teacher correction and evaluation, there are many reasons to believe that they can do a lot to improve writing. The entries may be considered one more form of improvisation that is to lead to a composition. Often material produced in the diary gives the student ideas for other writing assignments.

If some students feel that they have no idea what sort of things to put down in a diary, you can suggest that they use it to record some particular area or activity or relationship in their life—a sport, a job, a friendship.

If you work with the whole class or a group doing diaries at the same time, invite the diarists to talk about what it was like to keep a diary, how they felt about it, what things they may have noticed about the process itself or about the course of events as noted this way. Many very enlightening things may come out that can be of help to both teacher and student. Such a discussion is best played by ear, the teacher following up responses with impromptu questions that get the students to think more about their experiences and the way they verbalize. For instance, some may say that life is dull, too much the same from day to day. Since the latter can never be literally true, they may come to see how much our tendency to categorize things causes us to over-generalize, automatically, and leaves us with an impression of same-ness. Ask how some of these events look to them now; do they feel the same about them as they did the day of the entry? Why not? To whom were they addressing the diary? No one? Is that possible? To them-selves? Themselves when? Some find that they really had a particular person in mind. Why that person? How much did he or she influence what you wrote? Some find that they had an *image* of an audience of some kind, more or less local or general. These last questions might be correlated with the way they wrote the entries. Did they explain things and identify people and places even though they themselves knew? Did they provide links of thought and whole sentences as if for a reader other than themselves? Many students develop strong feelings about a diary. Pursue these. Some may say that keeping one helped them get things off their chest or cool off or change their mind about something. Without pushing too much, you might pursue the reasons why such things might happen just from writing.

Just as a matter again of sorting contents descriptively, ask a group of diarists if diaries tended to be full of events, or dominated by re-flections and questions, or focused mainly on descriptions of how they felt. Which direction does your diary go in? Did you find a lot of material that had little to do with the events of that day, that floated a bit out of time? Did present events trigger memories and general reflections?

Workshop Issues

With such questions ringing in the air, workshop groups might pre-pare for the following assignment by getting students to look at their diaries from a reader's point of view. What things would someone else not understand? Why not? What would you have to do if you were to make such things understandable? Which occurrences, descriptions, thoughts, and feelings would most interest other people if they were made understandable? Are there threads that run through the diary —strings of related events or connected thoughts and feelings? Students should bring their diary to class and take time in their group to look it over in the light of such questions. Encourage them to take marginal notations by way of answering them, when possible. Each could write a few sentences of commentary about what he sees now in his diary—things he hadn't noticed perhaps as he was keeping it, what he feels about some of the events now, what seems most interesting still, what threads and connections he sees, etc. Members of a group can agree to share diary contents indirectly by reading excerpts or summarizing passages. This gives diarists a chance to get advance reaction to material they are considering using if they can find a good way to edit it. Such a procedure could go on simultaneously with keeping the diary and would help students see how to draw material out for writing at any time. Partners can often suggest better ways of making notes and keeping entries for a given subject, as well as indicate what is interesting to them about whatever subject the diarist is tracking.

Related Activities

Since diary-keeping has many possibilities, and a lot of teachers today sponsor some form of it, it may be useful to make distinctions between log, journal, and diary and hence between variations of the basic experience of record-keeping. Let's say that a log is a rapid, impersonal noting of events in a rather systematic way, as with a police or ship's log. Groups or individuals in elementary school can keep a dated log on some project they have going, like a scientist keeping lab notes on an experiment. A journal, let's agree, is more specialized and less personal than a diary. We might use a journal to keep a running account of our observations of an ongoing activity or area of concern that we might or might not be directly involved in, and we would expect others to read entries. A diary is strictly for oneself and is a catch-all for anything that strikes the diarist as worthy of recording from day to day, including private feelings and commentary. It would be good for students to have experience with all three types. Primary children can make a calendar that has room to write on for each day and can put on it anything they want. Later they can differentiate the types above. One way to vary this assignment is to make it a journal, focused on one arena and open to others.

Younger students often want to share portions of their diary with the teacher but not necessarily with peers (though this is usually true only of youngsters who haven't had the experience of being in a writing group of some duration). Take some time to listen to or read these proffered excerpts, but suggest too that classmates might also want to hear some of them. Such kids need you, but they also need to be weaned. Your sitting in on groups can be the occasion to bring the two audiences together. If a group sets out to keep journals, they would presumably have an understanding at the outset that they would read each other's entries periodically (you too). There are gains and losses. Forsaking the intimacy of a diary means withholding some potentially good writing material, but sharing a journal along the way tends to stimulate a strong motivation to keep full entries and to think of the journal already as having an audience.

Encourage students interested in writing stories to try doing one by making up a diary. This intrigues many adolescents once they have been introduced to the idea and to some diary fiction. The form is fun to work with and can stimulate ideas that might not come any other way.

Collateral Reading

Experience as diarists will help students understand published diaries and fictional diaries as well as inspire them to seek these out. Real diaries are usually placed near or amid letters in public libraries. Explorers and adventurers often keep and publish diaries. Richard Henry Dana's classic *Two Years Before the Mast* is a diary. The diaries of George Washington, Christopher Columbus, Lewis Carroll, Thomas Edison, Queen Victoria, Anaïs Nin, Samuel Pepys, Fanny Burney, Ann Frank, and Vaslav Nijinsky, are among possibilities. See the log, diaries and journals in *Points of Departure*.

Part of *Robinson Crusoe* is a diary, and most of Goethe's *The Sorrows of Young Werther* is a diary, but modern novelists have used it more. André Gide's *Pastoral Symphony* may be the masterpiece of the genre, and the French have especially cultivated it: Jean-Paul Sartre's *Nausea*, George Bernanos' *Diary of a Country Priest*, and François Mauriac's *Nest of Vipers*. Good short stories for youngsters include Daniel Keyes' "Flowers for Algernon,"* Ring Lardner's "Diary of a Caddy" and "I Can't Breathe," Guy de Maupassant's "The Diary of a Madman," Nikolai Gogol's "The Diary of a Madman,"* William Harvey's "August Heat," Richard Matheson's "Born of Man and Woman," Donald Barthelme's "Me and Miss Mandible," and Mark Twain's "Extracts from Adam's Diary."

Students can apply their experience as diary writers to these stories to determine main connections among entries (plot or theme), the personality of the diarist, and changes in his state of mind and perspective. How would this story be different if it were all told from the vantage point of the last entry? Of years later? How different would it be if another character had told it through his diary?

Diary Summary

In 1000 to 1200 words write an account of the material covered by the diary. Feature both what seems of most importance to you and what you think will be of most interest to others. You are free to cut out and add material and to reorganize it. Don't use the dates; select and summarize so that you blend things into a continuous, whole piece.

The wording of this assignment expresses the main idea; many teachers might find a better way of casting it for their own students, and certainly it would have to be put differently to younger classes. Perhaps instead of a definite wordage, the length of the paper should be made proportionate to the length of the individual diary—say, one-third to one-half as long as the original. The crucial point is that the student should have to *digest* the diary, catch the essence of it while obliterating thoroughly the original form. This assignment is a natural lesson in composing, for it compels the student to determine what is salient, select accordingly, and organize around some notion of continuity and unity. Ideally, he would find some balance between the concreteness of raw details and the generality of a résumé.

Workshop Issues

A diary summary might lead to a first-person narrative such as one might write from memory; or to a character sketch of oneself; or to a personal essay structured by thought and feelings but illustrated by specific episodes or descriptions.

The *modes* of abstraction will vary according to the central concept that has guided the writer's selection and organization, which in turn may depend a lot on the contents of the diary; that is, some summaries will tend toward chronology, some toward a logical classification by, say, activities or concerns, and some toward a weaving of interrelated themes. These, and others, are all legitimate modes, and there is no reason to prefer one to another unless it seems inappropriate to the material or just plain dull.

Because of this possible spread, the reading and discussing of these papers could turn over many issues of narrative and exposition, but the case of this assignment is special in that it stems from a generous body of previously written material to which it was in some ways limited and to which it can be referred, at least in the mind of the student, who knows what decisions he made in getting from one stage to the other. Without revealing specifics of his diary, an author can talk about what changes he made in order to summarize. For example, if the summary would benefit from more dialogue, is the problem that he had no dialogue in the diary, or did he cut it? Is the summary so jumbled because he tried to do justice to everything in the original instead of selecting more narrowly? Did his diary contain so many thoughts and reactions to occurrences or did he add those later? In general, this type of question makes more sense when a group feels a weakness in the paper, but often tracing back the method of a successful paper will demonstrate to the other students what kinds of things we have to do to shape raw material into a good finished product.

The obvious challenge of a general diary is dealing with miscellany. In two ninth-grade classes where this assignment was once tried students came up with the following ways of organizing:

1. A snapshot technique—a selection of characteristic or special entries, revised and juxtaposed for effects of irony or slice-of-life.
2. A recurring event or situation cast into the present tense of generalization to show something typical.
3. One topic (sports, friends) singled out and traced or used to draw a conclusion.
4. Several categories of experience taken up one at a time, representing main aspects of the diarist's life during that period.
5. Development of a theme, drawing from material here and there without keeping time order.

Students in these classes, by the way, showed very strong interest in learning about each other's lives from these summaries, and this attraction seems pretty universal. None of the following samples benefited from workshop discussion.

Snapshot technique One girl chose the snapshot technique. She selected entries rather than items from entries, probably rewrote them somewhat, and juxtaposed them for a slice-of-life effect, obviously trying to exploit rather than overcome the miscellaneousness of the material.

There I stood staring at the building which seemed so strange and different to me. Although I had been going there for two years, it still seemed as if this day wasn't real. As I stood in front of the school, I saw faces of many people, some of whom I had known before and others were completely strange to me. Suddenly, I found myself walking up the stairs trying to find my way around. Then there it was my room number. I looked at it for a few minutes quite reluctant to enter. The numbers kept reappearing in my mind. I knew I must go in, and suddenly I was sitting down in the classroom a bit bewildered and lost. As the hours passed, I became accustomed to the teachers and my fellow classmates. There was much commotion that day. All the students were meeting new and happy faces, but there I stood trying to start a conversation which just wouldn't start. I finally got control of myself and got up enough courage to speak to a girl sitting next to me. The time seemed to pass quickly and when the bell rang for school closing I couldn't believe that it was over. I got my books and ran quickly out to catch the crowded bus. After some trampling over a tangle of feet, I made my way to the safety of a nearby seat.

What do you know? After much misgivings, I finally got to the dramatic school. I never thought that I would make it. There were about fifteen girls in the class and they all seemed friendly. Of course, there was always one stuffed shirt in the group. She thought that she could control the class. Then the teacher came in. She was a rather young looking woman. I looked at her suspiciously, in case she had thought that I was a good subject to deal with. It seemed as though I was here for at least a year, as the two hours seemed to drag on so slowly. Then it happened! I had to get up and pantomime a most ridiculous subject. Of course, I really didn't rebel in doing it; but it did seem kind of funny. Well, somehow the hours passed and with a sigh of relief I had gone through the first agony. From now on I won't be so self-conscious.

Today was art class and this was quite a relief from dramatics. This time at least I could do some independent creative work.

I won't be a great artist, but it won't hurt to try. My first picture didn't seem to look like anything very much, but with a few adjustments it might do as a "Rembrandt." The class was rather small. There were about six kids in the class. The kids were all nice and they really could draw well. My teacher was very nice and helped me with my drawings. What a mess! I got paint all over my good blouse. Well, I'd better be more careful next time. Soon the class ended and it was time to leave. It was now dark out and there stood my mother's car. I ran quickly to get in because it had just started to rain.[3]

Though she has not tried to face some of the tougher difficulties of the assignment, still this girl has written rather good accounts of bits of her experience. If nothing else, the assignment has elicited several personal narratives that seem to be written with interest. Not much abstracting has taken place, but the cutting was worthwhile.

Categories-of-experience organization The boy who wrote the following has assimilated and organized his material to a much greater degree, but the material is more meager, whether because he over-abstracted or because he simply did not keep a full diary, we don't know. His summary represents the categories-of-experience way of abstracting, which is effective here and also gives him a chance to talk about at least one important thing he has learned from his experience during the five weeks.

MY SUMMARY TO MY DIARY

The past five or six weeks if you count February vacation have been truly progressive for me. There are many miscellaneous happenings which would not interest you so I will not write about these, but I will discuss the general things that have been important to me.

The first and most important thing in my life has been grades. I've been trying or partially trying to boost my grades up and I have been succeeding in three subjects however, the other two I do not want to mention because some of you are in those classes with me. My main incentive has been a trip to California

[3] Weeks Junior High School, Newton, MA.

during the next vacation. Not for very long but it will be enough. I will be going by myself, and no one will be tagging along telling me what to do, which has been the tendency of my family in the five week span. My main obstacle for getting good grades is the dull routine, day after day. Go to school, come home, do homework, go to sleep, and go back to school the next day. It seems to me there must be a better way, but I guess no one has found it yet.

The second thing on my list has been my music. I have been in about four concerts in these five weeks, playing in the band and the orchestra, and I have one coming up this weekend with the band. The jazz combo to which I belong has begun to move, develop and really sound like something. Enough with the music. If I went on you'd get bored.

I have been on the swim team and I have really found out what its like to work for something. I had before but not to this extent. The reason I hadn't before was because my parents are not the very strict type and economically they haven't done too badly. But getting back to swimming, of course, I didn't make the first team but I did swim a couple of relays and I did swim in the I.V. meets. I found out what alot of boys are really like underneath because it comes out when he is tense and under the pressure of competition. I found that some kids who smoke and drink can really be good guys if they want to be and some kids who are maybe in A.P. and are real snob types can be real nice guys.

Also throughout my diary there are many places where it says I met someone today. I suppose this is a good sign. I don't know but I feel the more friends one has the better off someone is when he or she gets in trouble.

As a sort of conclusion I would like to say that Mrs. Lyon picked a great time for me to write a diary. I don't know about you but I've had a great time.[4]

The lack of detail, whether the fault of the diary or of the summary, would probably have been prevented if some of his colleagues had read his diary before the stage of composition. Working under a more significant title would also help.

---

[4] Lexington High School, Lexington, MA.

Thematic abstraction The excerpt from the boy's summary that follows represents one of the more sophisticated efforts to abstract meaningfully around themes, feelings, or ideas that, in retrospect, some of the incidents seemed to illustrate. One consequence is a mixture of generality and narrative, statement and example, which this boy carries much farther than the one who did the preceding paper: he has organized most of his summary around two stated themes, whereas the last diarist categorized his material by *areas* of experience (schoolwork, music, swimming) into which he inserted his general observation, for example, about boys under pressure. In both papers we can see the emergence of ideas and personal essay, which is one of the more promising turns that diary summaries can take. As an approach to essay, this assignment has the advantage of keeping generalizations in close relation to the actualities from which they were generated. This boy's generalizations are still very concrete and personal, but he is on the pathway to essay.

Somehow I always get myself into crazy situations by doing everything the hard way. This can be shown using the example of when the class had an assignment to catch flies for examination in biology.

We were supposed to have the flies in the next day, but that afternoon it was cool and cloudy. It wasn't a good day for flies because they like sunny days where they can sit on the concrete and sun themselves. Seeing that there were no flies to be netted on the concrete, I put some sugar water and raw meat outside in a jar for a few hours. That day turned out to a very bad one because I didn't even get any ants.

The next day I went to school without any flies. Nobody else had any either but there were a few bees brought in. It's frightening to look at bees through a magnifying glass which are sleeping off ether and can fly off at any minute. The next day we had to have flies or else.

We got out of school. I was getting my bicycle and I saw a nice big fresh mound of warm and smelly dog feces. I told one of my friends nearby. We didn't know if we would have an equal opportunity at home, so we went in and got some jars. We ended up with enough flies for the whole class, and the biology teacher was very happy with them, but this jubilance was neutralized when she picked up the jars and got dog feces all over her hands.

Another example of the way I go about everything the hard way is my method of getting notes for reports. Instead of going down three blocks to the local branch library, I go three miles on my bicycle to the main library because there are more magazines on world happenings there.

After I get home from school I only have one and a half hours for work because it takes half an hour to get to the library each way. Most of the time is wasted there because I spend most of my time looking for James Bond books, reading the electronics magazines, and looking at all the other things there.

I decided to spend a whole Saturday afternoon there so I didn't have to rush and could read more electronics magazines. I went with a friend on our bicycles. Halfway there I went through a shortcut which my friend didn't know much about but which I went all the time. He kept on going the long way and was going to meet me at our usual rendez-vous point.

Halfway through the shortcut in a desolated sidestreet my pedal suddenly fell off. For fifteen minutes I tried to screw it back on again.

I finally gave up and tried to ride my bicycle again. It was very difficult because you have to go at a good speed and the single pedal keeps on dropping down because it is off balance. I came to the rendezvous point, but my friend had already left so I went home to fix the pedal.

Halfway home I discovered I had a flat tire so I had to walk the rest of the way. It took two hours to fix the pedal and the flat tire, so in the end I had half an hour to go to the branch library. Doing everything the hard way gets you no further than if you didn't.[5]

The events of a diary can be viewed either as once-upon-a-time particulars or as instances of typical or general things. An important purpose of diary summary is to give students a chance to view them as both and thus to move away from pure narrative.

The "Diary Summary" differs from the next assignment mainly in that here the student isn't relying on memory, but neither does she have the perspective of time while writing: she is writing, as it were, from a lot of notes, and her vantage point is still close to the events when she summarizes the diary, not to mention when she is making

[5] Weeks Junior High School, Newton, MA.

the entries. So these papers have the advantage of strong recollection and the disadvantage of little perspective. We would expect, then, that many of them should seem biased and subjective to people other than the author. A great value of class discussion could be to get the students to make each other aware of their unconscious slant. For example, *X* may be trying to show that other people were to blame for certain things that happened to him, whereas it may be obvious to the class that the case is not so simple and that the author is rationalizing his own behavior. Or he may make a generalization that seems extreme to his classmates and is clearly based on a couple of particular experiences the author had that he has not yet got over.

Correcting perspective, however, is a delicate process; if the author is merely made to feel in the wrong, put at bay by the group, more than likely he will become defensive and dig in even more deeply into his position. The teacher must help workshop groups create an atmosphere that makes the individual feel helped, not attacked. Matching perspectives is the only way any person can achieve the awareness it takes to write well. Nobody listens to tirades for very long, and no reader can be persuaded by an author he sees through. It's quite enough if you can help students compare what they see with what others see. If an author can learn from that, he will. If he can't yet, it's no good trying to make him accept the view of others; it will, in fact, turn people against the workshop process.

Collateral Reading

Something that may help with this last issue is to read, while they are writing and discussing the diary summaries, several short stories told by a subjective narrator. There are many around, and frequently the character narrator is an adolescent. He or she recounts the events, or interprets them, in a way the reader sees through. Often the title suggests that the story is biased: "My Side of the Matter"* (Truman Capote), "Why I Live at the P.O."° (Eudora Welty), "My Sister's Marriage"* (Cynthia Rich), "I'm a Fool" (Sherwood Anderson), "You Should Have Seen the Mess" (Muriel Sparks), "My Old Man" (Ernest Hemingway), "The Loneliness of the Long Distance Runner"* (Alan Sillitoe), and "The Turn of the Screw" (Henry James). Moreover, various columns and articles in magazines and newspapers—especially "advice" columns—contain very one-sided accounts of events and situations. Students can bring in a number of these and discuss them. Do they sympathize with the plaintiff, or does his own account turn them against him? Often these are good for humor and can loosen up students about the universal difficulty of awareness and perspective.

So much of so-called reading comprehension is being able to size up the speaker and his attitude so that we can assess his story or ideas. Experience with unreliable or subjective speakers can help students a great deal. Bias, intentional and unconscious, is something students must become attuned to—in advertising and poetry, propaganda and fiction. They need to distinguish between the words and phrases in a student paper or reading selection that seem *calculated* to get the reader to see things a certain way and those words and phrases that look like "slips" or "give-aways." Do they feel they see something that Huck Finn or Holden Caulfield does not see in his own story?

Encountering fiction told by an imperceptive narrator raises the possibility for students both to write such stories deliberately themselves *and* to perceive how their own and each other's personal accounts, true or fictional, may indeed seem biased in exactly the same way as "You Should Have Seen the Mess." Such deliberately biased stories are much like many dramatic monologues, which rely on the same technique of self-exposure. In fact, writing deliberately biased material can become a very popular class sport among teenagers, along with detecting *unintended* bias and distortion in each other's writing. All of this helps overcome egocentricity. Interpreting of both real life and literature is involved. Consider in this dual way the following story, done by a senior in a class of mine at Exeter.

REQUIEM FOR A SUAVER

Ernie Finster was packing his bag when I came into the room (actually his name wasn't Ernie Finster, but his parents would give him hell if they ever knew that someone was writing about him and using the family name).

"Well, Ern, I just found out, if there is anything I can do, I'd be glad to—."

"Cool it, Roscoe, I think I can swing this one by myself." Old Ern always talked like that.

"Yeah, okay Ern. I just thought that there might be something I could do for you to sort of help pay you back for—."

"Yeah, well, man, now that you mention it, there is something that you could do for me. I've got a little package here for the dean. I wonder if you would mind slipping it under—."

"Hey, come on Ern, I can't do that. Ever since that time on the Howdy Doody show when you slipped me that package and then started yelling: "It's a bomb, it's a—."

"All right, all right, I get the message, can it. I just wanted to throw the suspicion off of me."

"Great. Right on to me. Super."

"All right, I said forget it. It was a poor idea anyway."

Ern put on his madras jacket and then took a quick look around the room to make sure that he had everything that he wanted. He stopped, gasped, ran over to his dresser and picked up a couple of dark blue capsules.

"Jesus Christ, I almost forgot my 4-X's."

He dropped the prophylactics in his jacket pocket, hauled the suitcase off the ground, and tramped out into the hall. Everyone who wasn't at the lacrosse game came out of his room to wish Ern good luck.

"See ya, Ern."

"Good luck, man."

"Take 'em easy."

"Swing gently, Ern boy."

"Etc."

Ern, of course, was not at a loss for an appropriate phrase. Climbing on top of his suitcase, he raised one madrased arm lyrically into the air.

"Albeit that I appear to be leaving you, for ever and ever, remark that the paths trod upon by the eternal suavers are few indeed. If not in Tel Aviv, then Madrid, or if not in Madrid, perhaps the Gold Coast. Just remember to keep your arms outstretched in widespread supplication to the gods, and who knows where or when they will bestow upon you the glory of my presence."

The applause and shouts of approval were deafening. Eager hands helped him down off the suitcase, clapped him on the back, and met with Ern's own in a last gesture of farewell.

After downing the two flights of stairs Ern and I left the dorm and headed for Front Street. The thought came into my mind that this was probably the last time that Ern would ever walk upon the old asphalt paths of dear Darby. It was a kind of sad thought, and I looked over at Ern to see if maybe he felt the same way that I did.

But of course, I should have known better. Old Ern was taking the whole thing in stride the way he always did. Nothing ever bothered old Ern. He was always the same, unchanging, stalwart picture of perpetual suavity. And it made me kind of laugh at my own, uncalled for, sentimentalism.

We got to where the bus was supposed to be, but of course,

in good old Darby tradition, it wasn't. So Ern and I sat down on the curb and waited.

After about a minute, Ern pulled out a tube and lit up. I was about to protest when I remembered that the school rules didn't apply to him any more. This thought reminded me of the reason for Ern's getting kicked out, which, I soon remembered, I didn't know. I wanted to ask him about it, but was afraid he would think it was a pretty wet question. After all, what difference did it make, in the long run, as far as the history of human existence was concerned?

But I asked him anyway, and it didn't seem to bother him too much at all.

"You know that big gray cat of Doc Spauldings? Well, I was drifting along back from the gym and I saw that big daddy standing out on Doc's lawn, just staring at me, great big cool looking eyes, you know, just staring. And I thought, 'Jesus Christ,' would that motha look suave with a California lean; like a hot rod, you know. So I picked up the Doc's hedge clippers, which happened to be lying on the grass, and chopped off the cat's back legs, about half way up. It was really wild. You should have seen that daddy running around on his stumps. Christ, it nearly killed me. Anyway, the cat ran into the house bleeding like a motha, and about thirty seconds later, Spaulding's old lady comes bombing out screaming for the cops and the militia, and god knows what else. Christ, she never shut up. I turned around and started walking back to the dorm, but only got about a hundred yards before old Twinkie Parsons came running up from behind, grabbed me and dragged me back to the scene. Voila."

"Suave, Ern," I said, knowing it must be, "but why did you do something like that?" (Not that it was any more unusual than anything else that he did, but it seemed to be not quite in the same good taste in which he usually acted. In fact, it smacked of a different Ern altogether, and I was curious.)

"I had a pet rabbit once when I was seven, by the name of Flopsy. One day my mother told me to build a cage for him and put him outside because he was stinking up the house. I built one out of a cardboard box, and I guess that it wasn't very strong. Anyway, the first night he was out our neighbors' cat broke into the cage and tore him into little pieces. I sat there for five hours trying to put him back together."

If old Ern hadn't immediately burst out into his tremendous rolling laugh, I would have thought that he had slipped his trolley. I think that I laughed even harder than he did. Good old Ern, he's a million yuks.

The bus came around the corner and stopped in front of us. Ern stood up, slipped into his imported French shades, and mounted the bus. He paid the driver and then turned and nodded to me in a kind of final acknowledgment of our friendship. I raised my hand in sort of a half salute and smiled. Ern turned and walked down the aisle, stopping long enough to put his bag in the rack before slipping in beside some gorgeous college broad. I saw her look up at him kind of surprised like, as if she knew exactly what he was after; and then I laughed, because, as the bus pulled away, I knew that it didn't really matter if she knew or not.

The narrator's worship of his suave hero falters only for a moment —after the cat story—but he recovers and reaffirms his faith in good ol'Ern, because he needs to. If, like the author of the story, he were to see Ern as a very sick boy, he would be lost; he would have to renounce the whole James Bond, schoolboy mystique that he believes he lives by. Though this invented narrator may very well be the author as he was a couple of years before, he is distinctly not the boy who wrote the story. From first sentence to last, the author has made sure that the reader will know one from the other.

On the nonliterary side, suppose that other students who read "Requiem for a Suaver" worship the Erns of their world. They are unaware of the story's irony. This is precisely how personal values and private understanding of experience determine how one interprets what one reads, whether in fiction or nonfiction. No amount of literary knowledge can prevent someone from reading a subjective narration as an objective memoir or autobiography. Literature always breaks back ultimately into life. Seldom do more involved or fruitful discussions take place than those about amateur and professional stories narrated by teenagers whose perspective is transitional between stages of maturity.

Autobiography: Incident

Tell an incident that happened to you some time in the past, an incident being a specific occurrence that took place only once, on a certain day or perhaps covering a couple of days. (800– 1000 words.) To be printed and distributed in an Autobiography: Incidents booklet.

Although a number of previous assignments should have prepared for this, perhaps the most directly relevant one is the Spontaneous Memory Monologue, which can be done again now as a primer—and whenever helpful for other writing. The assignment itself bears repeating very well and can be used to look back at different periods of one's life. This assignment serves too as a model for writing short stories featuring an incident and told by the person to whom the incident occurred. These incidents can also make excellent poems.

Workshop Issues

Their selection of an incident implies automatically some kind of importance or point to it. But the student may not understand himself at first what the significance of the incident was; all he knows is that it stands out or "left a strong impression." The reasons why it stood out or impressed him, if understood and brought into play somehow, will usually invest the paper with significance and interest for others. Otherwise it will seem pointless. Therefore, the major task of the workshop with this assignment is to help students get the real experience to emerge, or to help them try to understand why it did not. If this issue is central, some of the techniques or skills of writing narrative should be easier to deal with, since the point, impression, or significance of the incident dictates the choices about how to tell it, and governs the whole. The same applies to all of the following assignments calling for *retrospective* narrative, drawing on real-life material.

Since *the order of actions is given* by the facts of the case, the student exercises judgment only in choosing *which* actions to relate and which to omit, which to expand in detail and which to summarize in passing. These are matters we usually call focus and emphasis, but they are factors of personal selection and attention. There is no "pure narrative." The student's judgment also determines whether he will supply background information, and, if so, when—in a chunk at the beginning, or at the end, or bit by bit along the way. The third thing which is *not* given in the original events is interpretation, the necessity of which the student has to decide, and also the method of getting this in—by weighted word choice, by sheer dwelling of attention, or by direct commentary. Should point and significance be merely implied, or is the story going to require some abstract statement?

Responders should ask themselves: What does the narrative feature? What do things seem to point to? What does the narrative *do*? How did the student choose to tell this? Note where he began and ended the action. Did he explain much? Can responders tell his attitude or how he felt? Are attitude and feeling clear because he makes direct statements or because they are implied in words and phrases?

An issue of general value that this assignment raises is how much the author features himself and how much he focuses on other people or things. Although the assignment calls for autobiography, an incident that could be said to have "happened to" the author, the emphasis will undoubtedly vary a lot in these papers, and there is no reason to make a student feel wrong who has, in fact, written a piece of eyewitness reportage or a fragment of memoir or biography; the main thing is that the group or the teacher help him become *aware* of his emphasis. Pointing out in discussion those papers that subordinate the speaker to some other subject has the advantage of demostrating the distinction upon which other assignments are based as well as clarifying generally both (1) such classifications as autobiography, memoir, firsthand reportage, and biography, and (2) the fictional techniques that parallel these kinds of narratives. Certainly it's not always easy to distinguish one from the other—where the greatest emphasis lies—partly because one's own experience is closely tied to that of other people, and also because observing is itself sometimes *quite* an experience, especially if one is involved in the subject and reacting strongly to it. But it's important for the student to try to discriminate, in his own and in other's writing, between a speaker-centered story, an other-centered story, and a dual-centered story. A student should know when he is featuring what he means to feature, and he should be able to perceive what another writer is placing *his* emphasis on.

Collateral Reading

What will help both the writing and the reading comprehension of narrative is to read along with this whole series of first-person narrative assignments a number of short stories and narrative poems either arranged so as gradually to shift the focus off the narrator onto other people or things or else jumbled so as to force the student constantly to decide who or what the focus is on. There is also a wealth of nonfictional first-person narrative to accompany all of these assignments—current magazine articles, true stories, books of autobiography, memoir, and reportage. For older students, *The New Yorker* affords a perennial source of first-person writing of all sorts, but teen magazines and many other popular periodicals provide plenty of unsophisticated counterparts. Some of the most accessible poems, such as many of Robert Frost's, are incidents of autobiography abstracted in such a way as to achieve universality. The *Reader's Digest* always features autobiographical incidents. Have students look for and clip out of newspapers and magazines the autobiographical incidents they see and like. All published autobiographies are full of them, of course, like Sandra Pisneros's *Ghosts and Special Voices: Writing from Obsession* and Ernest Galarza's *Barrio Boy.*

Some short stories are based on an incident. Consider classics like William Carlos Williams' "The Use of Force,"* John Updike's "A & P,"* and Frank O'Connor's "First Confession."* For examples from real life done by students, see *Active Voices.*

Autobiography: Phase

Tell what happened to you during a certain period of your life covering many months, perhaps even a year or so—some "phase." (1500 to 2000 words.) To be printed and distributed in an Autobiography booklet with other of your pieces or those of classmates.

A major task of this assignment is to distill, without losing vividness, the events that spread over a large extent of time and perhaps space. Like the "Diary Summary," this task draws on abstractive powers and organizing abilities, with the difference that the student must rely on memory in lieu of "notes." His perspective can only be that of the present except to the degree that he can successfully recall the perspective of the time he is writing about. Like Autobiography: Incident, this assignment can be varied by directing the student to different periods of his life. But the essential problem is to abstract a lot of raw material in a meaningful way. Making up a first-person story—an assignment that might follow this one—does not entail the same process at all, for the things that have actually happened are givens that must be worked with.

Workshop Issues

Although much of what was said about the last assignment holds also for this one, the value of working with a larger time-space scope is that decisions about selection, emphasis, and central concept are more difficult. Also, summarizing more material makes retaining vividness a more sophisticated skill. Thus, the two main issues which differentiate this assignment and which the workshop might use as a guide in discussion are: What idea of "phase" does the student use as his criterion for relevance in selecting and emphasizing? And what efforts does he make or fail to make to offset the abstractness of summary? The papers should not read like entries in an encyclopedia—résumés of fact with no concrete qualities of the original events and feelings. And yet, if the student narrates too much in detail, quotes too often, and stays entirely in moments of the past, he cannot come near telling what happened over a period of months.

The crux of the assignment, then, lies in some balance between precise actualities—what people did, said, felt, etc.—and some encompassing idea, a notion of a trial gone through, a stage of growth experienced, a set of circumstances lived through, a relationship developed. This idea may or may not need to be directly stated, depending on how obvious it will be to the reader—not always an easy thing to guess in advance. As for vividness, this calls for shrewdness about when to pull in for a close-up of a certain scene and when to summarize in a few sentences the less important or repetitive events. Although necessarily abstract in its condensation, a summary need not be abstract in its language. A general statement about what occurred "in the meantime," or what occurred habitually over a period of weeks, can be cast into concrete words and phrases, specific references. A well-chosen passage from a novel can demonstrate very well this particular art. Almost any reaction at all will involve these problems of abstracting and of writing narrative that this assignment is designed to raise, but most students will not see the problems as we have stated them. What you can do when sitting in on a workshop is follow up vague or subjective reactions with a question that makes the student reacting think more specifically about what the author did or didn't do that got the result he responded to.

Sample The following phase of autobiography was written by a boy who came to Phillips Exeter Academy for one year as a senior, having already graduated from a Greater Boston high school the year before.

When I was in the fifth and sixth grades, my mother wanted me to become an altar boy. I disliked the idea before I even knew what it was all about, and when I knew, I disliked it even more. Every Saturday morning when everybody else was out skating, I had to go to church and try to learn how to answer the priest in Latin. There were about thirty boys in the class, whose mothers had also made them come to the lessons. They all claimed that they were never prepared for the lessons, but

it was evident that their mothers had made them study the Latin during the week. My mother had tried also, but it just would not sink in, mainly because I did not want it to. I hoped that I could prove to both my mother and our priest that I was too dumb to learn how to serve mass. When I was called on in class, I would stand up and give a phrase I had heard somebody else give earlier in the lesson. The kids thought it was kind of funny giving the right answer to the wrong question. Sometimes if he called on me two or three times I would give the same answer. Once he got mad at me and asked me if I was trying to be funny. I denied it and told him that it simply was the only response I knew. That afternoon he called my mother and told her that if I did not have my lessons prepared in the future and continued to disrupt the whole class, I would have to give up the idea of being an altar boy.

Every afternoon that week my mother had me come in and study that foolish Latin. In the evening she would make me recite what I was supposed to have learned. My brother by this time had learned more Latin than I had. He would just sit there and listen every evening. When I did not know the answer, he would give the responses to my mother. This would always bring on the old song and dance about why couldn't I do it if my little brother could. The answer was that I did not want to learn it, and he did. He enjoyed making a fool of me, so every night that he tried to humiliate me when I went over the lesson, I would beat him up. He would scream and run to my mother, and she in turn would beat me. It was a losing battle and I was always on the short end.

Eddie had shown such deftness for Latin that she thought that he too would make a fine altar boy. On Saturdays, my brother would know the Latin as well as any of the older boys in the group. He had slaved all week just to show his stupid brother up, and I knew it. All was not lost, however, because I too knew my Latin. The priest was amazed and thought that if I could learn the Latin, then surely his class was making fair progress. Actually what I did was to have a friend of mine in the class sit in front of me, and I pinned the Latin card to his back. When I was called to write, all I did was read it off his back. The reason I was able to get away with this was that the priest did not know the Latin either, and as I was writing the priest was looking at his missal to see if I was saying it correctly. I really made fine strides this way. Every week I knew the Latin. Everything was going fine until one morning I read the priest's response on the card instead of the altar boy's. Everybody started to laugh because they all knew what I was doing. What really finished it was my friend made the mistake of turning around to laugh at me. When he did, the priest saw the Latin card that was pinned to his back. He did not say much, he just came down and tore the card off the boy's back, and my friend told him that he did not know that it was on there. The one who had a lot of talking to do was Eddie. He made sure he got home to tell his version of the story first. My mother was really mad, and screamed at me for about ten minutes. She finally hit me on the nose because I started to hum and tap my foot while she was trying to give me what she called constructive criticism. So with a bloody nose, I took my brother's skates out into the back yard and pounded the blades against the fireplace until they were too dull to ever try to skate on. My father was not too mad that I had used a bit of outside help in my Latin assignments. In fact, I think he thought it was a little humorous but did not show it openly.

The following Saturday there was a final written test in Latin. I asked the priest if I could go into the next room because it was quieter. When I got in there I took out my father's missal that I had taken from his bureau, and copied down all those responses that I had to know. Then I turned to the back of the book and answered all the questions about the priest's vestments. I did not care about cheating. I just wanted to show up my brother. Well, I passed with flying colors and substantially outdid my brother. When my brother and I served our first mass, my brother would answer the priest so loud that anybody in the church could hear him. I just mumbled except when all we had to say was "Amen." I liked the funerals best of all because they were usually on school days. The funerals in our church were usually at nine or ten in the morning, so we would have the whole morning off. I had a friend from school who was also an altar boy and asked to serve on the same funerals so we could walk to school together. His mother had told him to stay away from me, but he did not mind getting into trouble either.

When the funeral was over, we would walk as slowly as we could the mile to school. We used to stop along the way to ride a donkey or chase sheep. When we got to school, if it was too early, we would sit in the woods until lunch time and then go in. I was an altar boy until I was in the eighth grade, when I was thrown out because of fighting in the church. We weren't really fighting. We were just rolling around on the altar when we were supposed to be practicing for a wedding.

Most of the time my parents are hard to get along with, but during that year they were unspeakable. My father kept me in almost every Friday and Saturday night for something I had done either at school or at home. I did not mind getting in trouble for something I had done that was really wrong, but some of the things I was kept in for made me fight my parents even more.

Friday night would find me reduced to watching television for not making my bed, being late for breakfast, or hitting my little sister. One of the worst was having to stay in for not untying my shoes before taking them off. My father would come into my room every night after I was in bed to check my shoes. Just for spite I used to take them off and untie them. I could not stand my parents during those years and neither could my friends. They would not come into the house because I was always fighting with them.

I was playing varsity hockey that year, and my father even kept me out of some of the games. He would take my skates away for a week at a time for some really stupid reason. The only reason I was kept on the team was that the coach missed the same games I did. Our coach was Butch Songin and at that time he was playing quarterback for the Boston Patriots.

I tried to live in my own world. When I came home from skating I would go up to my room and only come down for meals. If I was watching television or sitting in the den and my father walked in I would get up and leave just to avoid an argument.

Things got progressively worse at home and at school. I was not doing much of anything. In February my father decided to bring me into Boston University to take a battery of tests given as a course of guidance. They told me I was there to see what courses in school would fit me best, but I knew I was there because my parents wanted to know if I could do the work I was supposed to be doing and if I could why wasn't I? The tests were the type in which you play with blocks, puzzles and ink spots. Also, someone would flash pictures in front of you and ask you what was the first thing that came into your mind. At the end of the thirty-hour testing period they came to the conclusion that I was quite bright but had difficulty in reading and spelling. My scores ranged from a perfect score in abstract reasoning to about twenty-five percent in reading and spelling. They also told my father to lay off me and in this way I would come along myself because I would not be fighting them. However, the next term he went back to his old suppression because I came home with two D's and two E's.

About this time I got sick of everyone, my teacher and my parents. The teachers were really wearing on me, and I thought that our priest was the most two-faced person I knew. During the football and hockey seasons everything was fine with him. But as soon as hockey was over he too started to climb on my back. I got very fresh and gave everyone a hard time, even teachers that were the type not to fool around with. One teacher used to talk about a certain element in the room that should be removed. So now I was an element: she even called me an element of refuse. One day when she was talking about this "certain element" I started to laugh. She got so red I thought she would explode. She started to cry and said until I left the room she would not come back in. I sat in the class all day while she sat out in the hall, where she had moved her desk. I was not going to leave. I would have stayed there for the rest of the year and the following if I had to. The next day her things were back in the room. She publicly proclaimed that either I left the school that year or she would. That summer she left.

This sample illustrates several additional issues that the assignment should engage students with. One is the transition from chronological organization to a thematic organization by ideas. Most accounts of a phase combine narrative with essay. That is, either the paper generally progresses chronologically but contains topical paragraphs in which time stands still while a general point is made, or the progression is a development of general points illustrated by bits of narrative taken out of chronological order. These organizations naturally occur because autobiography has the double goal of telling what happened while summarizing in a meaningful way. Before revising, students should try to decide, with a given paper, what presentation is best.

If you will look back over the sample above, you will notice that the level of abstraction varies considerably, according to whether the author is recounting a single incident that happened only once, summarizing recurrent or typical events, or describing a general situation. In a rough way the paper moves from the time he began learning to be an altar boy until the summer the teacher left (the exact period of time covered being not very well indicated, as a matter of fact). The result is not a narrative in the sense of a series of events; it is an account of a worsening situation or relationship, illustrated by events and marked by events, but not fastened down to particularities in precise order. How he prepared his lessons, how his brother tried to show him up, what he did on funeral days, the way he and his family behaved toward each other, the spread of hostility toward other adults—these are situations or stages that he usually introduces by more abstract sentences of the sort that teachers have been fond of calling topic sentences but which are generated spontaneously by the very needs of the assignment.

The second matter is time perspective. What enabled this boy to disengage a thematic unity from the welter of past facts was a certain emotional distance. From a remoter vantage point one can see patterns. Autobiography is characterized by binocular vision: the writer splits into I-now and I-then, which means that he looks at events from the remembered viewpoint of the past and from his present viewpoint. In the sample above, for example, though the boy says his parents *are* hard to live with, still it is obvious that he would have given a vastly different account of those earlier years if he had not changed considerably since then (as indeed he had). For one thing, an account written at the time could hardly have been so intentionally funny or so devoid of anger and self-justification. It is remarkably "objective."

When we say that *Great Expectations* is told from Pip's point of view, or *To Kill a Mockingbird* from Scout's, we mean, of course, that they are told from the points of view of two middle-aged narrators who have framed their childhood perspective within their later perspective. Compare *Catcher in the Rye*, narrated a year after the events, with *A Separate Peace*, narrated fifteen years later. How well a student succeeds in defining themes, then, will depend partly on how far he stands from the events in time. Discussions of papers should allow for time lapses and consequent perspectives. Personally, how one abstracts his past is critical, for the basic function of abstracting is to guide action. The very effort to write large-scope autobiography may help to induce a maturer perspective, as perhaps it did for the boy here.

Collateral Reading

Libraries and bookstores are filled with autobiographies. Let students choose personages and help them try to find their autobiographies. Many youngsters want to read about role models, their heroes and heroines, or other figures they want to identify with or want to check out. In addition to chestnuts like Helen Keller's autobiography, there are Richard Wright's *Black Boy*, Gordon Parks' *A Choice of Weapons*, Maya Angelou's *I Know Why the Caged Bird Sings*, Mickey Mantle's *The Education of a Baseball Player*, Sybil Leek's *Dairy of a Witch*, *Davy Crockett's Own Story*, *Sugar Ray*, Charles Lindergh's *We*, Agnes de Mille's *Dance to the Piper*, Richard Rodriguez's *Hunger of Memory*, Piri Thomas's *Down These Mean Streets*, Yevgeny Yevtushenko's *A Precocious Autobiography*, and literally hundreds or thousands more that youngsters would enjoy. Excerpts in *Points of Departure* from such books are "My Name Is Margaret"° by Maya Angelou and "Mucho Days and Nights in Gray"° by Piri Thomas. Short, self-contained autobiographical experiences are "The Scrolls, Too, Are Mortal"° by Elie Wiesel and "Besieged"° by Jessie Benton Frémont.

Autobiographical novels—told, that is, as if by the protagonist—include Charlotte Brontë's *Jane Eyre*, Charles Dickens' *Great Expectations* and *David Copperfield*, Ernest Hemingway's *A Farewell to Arms*, J.D. Salinger's *The Catcher in the Rye*, Ralph Ellison's *Invisible Man*, Chaim Potek's *The Chosen*, Warren Miller's *The Cool World*, Richard Brautigan's *In Watermelon Sugar*, and Joseph Krumgold's *And Now Miguel*. Edgar Lee Masters' *Spoon River Anthology* is a series of capsule autobiographies uttered beyond the grave and written as poems.

Memoir: Human Subject

Recount some memory that involved other people. Recreate it as you learned of it and include the reactions you had at the time. To print up in a booklet. (1000 to 1200 words.)

Although, by accomodating an incident again, this assignment seems to reverse our trend toward a larger scope of time and space, it requires further abstractive development of another sort. Reporting what happened to others entails more *inference*. The significance of events we merely observe, of what befalls someone else, is something we must guess at: we often have to get background circumstances from other people, and especially we do not know what the others felt or thought. Only by drawing on possible *similarities* in our own experience, or in invoking previously made categories and generalities, can we find meaning in our observation of others. Whatever point a student sees in some incident he reports will depend on how he classifies behavior. Whatever inferences he makes about the inner experience of the participator or about the general meaning of the events will depend on a risky but necessary abstractive operation. It is mainly this particular operation that distinguishes this assignment from other first-person narrative. Otherwise, the issues are the same as those sketched in the previous two assignments.

A similar account might be obtained by going to some place for the express purpose of reporting what one sees there, as indicated in "Composed Observation." Though results may look alike, the compositional issues differ markedly between writing from sensory notes and writing from memory. Having the intention before one observes affects the eyewitnessing, whereas in recalling, one is subject to the laws of memory operating on adventitious material. A diary entry might contain the kernel for such a paper.

Keep reminding writers that they can fictionalize such incidents by making up additional material and by altering how things happened, or that they can invent a whole episode. Naturally, the workshop can't treat fictional eyewitness as if the author had been limited to what he once beheld, so fiction ought to be identified at some point.

The personal memory that follows was written by a girl in eleventh grade.[6] The protagonist is her brother; she is both confidant and eyewitness. However, since she was not present at all the events, she has to tell some of it as it was told to her. This kind of very involved but peripheral narrator is the "first person" of most published memoirs.

MEMORY OF MY BROTHER ACCIDENT

The most terrifying thing that ever happened to me was on December 24, 1962. My second brother was shot with a 16 ga. shotgun. At the time he was fourteen years old. This is the way it happen. My brother James and cousin (N. C. Mayers.) went hunting around 1:00 o'clock that morning of the day he got shot. N. C. was behind James. N. C. had his gun loaded as they was walking along. James shouted, "Look, there is a squirrel." At that instant N. C. pulled the trigger on his gun. The bullets hit my brother's left hand below his elbow. This James walked along for about ten minutes. Meanwhile N. C. had stopped and was staring in disbelief. James finally went to hold up his hand and said, "Man, look, my hand has been shot," and he only looked and said, "They're going to cut my hand off." Then he walked on to my uncle's house and said, "Uncle Mob, open the door I been shot." My uncle didn't believe him because he had been carrying on a lot of foolishness. After about five minutes of convincing my uncle, he finally open the door and stared in horror at the blood and the condition of James' hand. My uncle

---

6 With thanks again to Charles Thurow, director of English for an Upward Bound program at Tougaloo College, MS

was tall, dark, around 65 years old. He lived in a three room house on his farm about twelve miles from civilization. He told James to set down and gave him a sheet to put his hand in while he go down to the barn and hitch his mules to the wagon because he didn't have any other mean of transportation.

It took Uncle Mob about 15 minutes to drive from his house to ours in a wagon. After Uncle Mob and James get to the house my parents was at work and had the car. All of us came out of the house and looked at James in horror, but James was smiling. Then we all begin to cry and scream. My oldest brother got on the horse and at no time at all he got my cousin to take James to the hospital. He took him to Brandon Hospital, but the doctors there said they had to cut his hand off, but the university hospital in Jackson might could save it so they took him to the University. I cannot give a description of the hospital nor doctor because I wasn't there. By this time my uncle had notified my parents and they were there. The doctor asked my mother permission to cut his hand off and she refused. He explained to her that wasn't but two leaders holding his hand together and the arm will never be anymore good anyway. My mother still refused so the doctors took him into surgery and sewed his leaders together and put his arm in a cast for six weeks. After the six week period they put his hand into a mending bandage for four more weeks. After the four weeks period they left his arm bare, which didn't look so good, but he still had it and after a short time he started using his left hand as good as his right hand. And now, which is four years later, my brother still thanks my mother for not signing the paper.

My cousin N. C. went out of his head for about two days. He didn't come home and didn't say anything to anyone because he thought we would blame him for what happen. Two years after the accident N. C. died of pneumonia and someone had stab him with an ice pick.

Workshop Issues

In addition to using this assignment to continue work on narrative in general, the group can exploit, in discussion and commentary, what is unique about it. First, establish how close to or remote from the principal figure(s) the author was, how much previous knowledge he did or did not have of them, and how much he was dependent on just what he saw and heard that particular time. How detached or involved is he? Did he *become* more involved? What was it that "drew him in?" How did he react to what he witnessed? Would you have reacted the same way? Would you have interpreted or categorized the action as he did? It's very important to draw attention to inferences. How does the author know what he did not witness or previously know? Does he attempt to say what the inner experience was of the other people? Was he right, in your opinion?

The point of all this is not to make the student gun-shy about hazarding inferences—after all, we must and do all the time, and many deep and moving accounts issue from such risks—but to help him see the risk and to so strengthen his judgment and perspective that he will gamble well. Often a memoir turns out to be unwitting autobiography, either because the student focused more on himself and his feelings than he thought, or because the significance he saw was too subjective, i.e., *unawarely* private. Exploring this sensitive area can leave the author feeling that he has gained, not lost. If the tone of discussion is collaborative and supportive, and if the tradition is that we grow by matching and comparing perspectives, students should not be burned badly by having an interpretation questioned. Usually the reactions and interpretations are what make for the best writing in memoir, and purely objective accounts are hardly possible anyway: the issue is whether the writer is capitalizing on his reactions or whether they are unwittingly and subjectively determining what he says.

Collateral Reading

Some of the somewhat fictionalized sketches from Ivan Turgenev's *Sportsman's Notebook,* such as "The Tryst"* and "The Singers,"° afford beautiful samples of this assignment and will appeal to students much more if offered as memoir than as short stories. Magazines and newspapers often run memoirs of people whose experience figures into current concerns. But, especially, let students browse library memoir shelves.

Walter van Tilburg Clark's novel *The Ox-Bow Incident,* popular with youngsters, is told as memoir by a minor character, as are Poe's "The Fall of the House of Usher,"* and O'Henry's "Municipal Report."

Memoir: Nature

Give an account of some action you witnessed in which people played no part. Give your own thoughts and reactions, however. To be printed. (1000 words.)

Although this assignment is essentially only a variation of the last, it's nevertheless very important to single out because it asks for an informal kind of scientific writing—something that is seldom done in English but should be. Any of the later assignments about generalizing and theorizing from firsthand and secondhand information could be used to foster scientific writing. Further, a student who wanted to specialize his diary could make it into a journal of birdwatching or geological exploration or experimentation.

Whereas we have the advantage, in writing about people, of being kin to them and of understanding them, at least generally, from the inside, we are in much greater ignorance about the causes and the meaning of what we observe in the rest of nature—unless, of course, we have acquired information from the past about insect behavior, the motion of stars, or the chemistry of plant life. The papers produced by this assignment may well range from personal, poetic response to nature to clinical and quantitative reportage, but they would logically all be some kind of narrative. Papers distributed to the class could sample this range.

Experiments with this assignment in eighth grade produced a remarkable number of truly interesting accounts. These showed clearly that the students really enjoyed doing it and welcomed an opportunity to write on a subject they felt very involved with. The world of animals and live landscapes exerts a strong pull on youngsters even through puberty. Some might like to make up animal and nature stories based on observations they have made.

The breakers crashed the rocks and ran away with a hissing sound. The gray sand was dotted with birds' prints. It was a bleak November day at the beach, dark save for the thin watery sunlight breaking through the clouds. The wind whistled through the waving dune grass and made white-caps on the waves.

Suddenly the peaceful silence was broken by a flock of hungry sea gulls flying over head, hunting food. There was a bag of garbage left on the beach by some careless picknicker, and the gulls, smelling this delicacy, were already landing around it. After a few minutes the scene had turned into a complete battle. Squaks, screeches and the swoosh of wings accompanied this "tug-of-war" combat which involved the survival of the fittest. Food was pulled between beaks, stepped on and sent flying into the rumbling ocean.

Two particular gulls, I noticed, were engaged in a life or death wing-to-wing combat. There was an old strong gull who looked like he'd been through many similar episodes like this, and a young brown-speckled gull. The young one had what looked like a moldy sandwich and was contentedly pecking at it, not bothering a soul. The old sly bird spied this jealously and made up his mind to get it. He opened his large beak and snapped at the diner's tail so hard that the younger jumped away from his dinner. The other, seeing its' chance, grabbed the morsel and flew to a nearby jetty. After recovering from its shock the brown-specked bird in his anger began to circle round the other greedy gull and finally swooped down hitting him hard. There, silhouetted against the gray sky the two birds fought, not a playful romp, but a fight which meant the loser would forfeit a rare meal, for there was little to eat these cold days. One may even be killed, because if there was a sea gulls manual, they were using every trick in the book. The sandwich lay barely touched next to the hysterical birds. All the other gulls had flown off satisfied or to seek out more food, but these gulls continued their ordeal. The younger was beginning to weaken and the other would jab at him fiercely when he paused. Blood was flecked on the older's white breast, but he was not losing strength. Finally, when the younger looked too weak to even eat the food, the other gave him one fierce push that sent him tumbling off the jetty, and landed, a crumpled heap in the water. The poor thing apparently had broken it's wing and now he was at the mercy of the angry sea. He bobbed a few times, gasping but finally disappeared in the inky ocean. The sly bird, happy with his victory snatched the sandwich in his beak and started to fly away. But, suddenly against the sky I saw his figure falling into the sea for he was too tired to carry the food and fly. The sea gull joined his enemy undersea.[7]

Workshop Issues

Given our relative lack of affinity with physical things and lower orders of life, the chief issues concern how to understand what we are witnessing and how to sustain reader interest without "human interest." Suggest to a group that they look for and call attention to the

[7] From Weeks Junior High School, Newton, MA. The teacher was Eugenia Nicholas.

different ways its members have tried to solve these problems—by a marked personal point of view, the feeding in of pertinent information culled elsewhere, or an effort to relate the observed events to human nature and behavior.

An aware and imaginative comparison of nonhuman to human affairs usually makes for good writing, and, as we know from the example of the best scientific writers, well chosen metaphors can illuminate and enhance scientific understanding. Comparisons between nonhuman and human clearly provide a main way of understanding nature and giving it meaning and interest. Here an important distinction has to be made between *tuning in* to nature and *projecting into* nature. Fine naturalists clearly have more affinity with nature than other people and hence can better explain it and make it interesting. It's not always easy to know what is insight and what is projection. People naturally see anthropomorphically, treat other things and creatures as if they were like us. But in many ways, they *are* like us, because certain aspects of nature are common to everything, and everything is ultimately related to everything else. Small children will anthropomorphize automatically, because they are still just learning to distinguish the self from the rest of the world anyway. Adults too often want to rub this out as being unrealistic and unscientific, but animating nature and investing it with human traits make up part of childhood and fade anyway. Poets deliberately employ anthropomorphism to help us relate to and appreciate what we really are a part of anyway. I would never try to correct youngsters' views of what they see in nature, but I think that *peers* would gain a lot from discussing whether an author intends his comparison between human and nonhuman to be the truth or merely a metaphor. Help the *students* to thrash this out among themselves. Their own discussion will make them aware that they are seeing and taking things differently and that comparing may be regarded literally or metaphorically. How should they take their anthropomorphism? If you help them just to engage with that, you have done your job.

Collateral Reading

For many students, "action" or "event" may mean only rapid movement on a large scale. To offset this limited notion as well as to introduce them to some of the relevant literature of nature observation, acquaint them with Karl von Frisch's *Bees: Their Vision, Chemical Senses, and Language*, Henry David Thoreau's *Walden*, and the books of Gerald Durrell, John Muir, Farley Mowat, Peter Mathiessen, Annie Dillard, and Anne Morrow Lindbergh. The games of dogs, changes of weather, flight patterns of birds are all "actions." "Battle Tactics"° by Farley Mowat is a good example. *Ranger Rick,* the *National Geographic, National Wildlife, Audubon,* and *Natural History* contain eyewitness accounts of nature.

Variations of Memoir

Memoirs can go on and on, shifting from incidents to phases, as we did with autobiography, and varying focus from individuals to groups, from people to nature, and from subjects close to remote from the narrator. "Memoir" merges gradually into "Biography" and "Chronicle," covered later in this progression.

Reporter-at-Large

Go visit some place of business or other enterprise, talk with people there, watch its operation, take notes, then write an account of the visit afterwards. Use your narrative to convey a lot of information about the enterprise, to catch the atmosphere of the place, and to show what the people there are like. To print and distribute. (2000 words.)

This is an omnibus assignment in that it brings together several different kinds of writing that the student has been practicing. It involves recreating some of the dialogue of the interview, recounting actions, describing appearances of things, and exposing facts. Having received some data directly through his senses and other data in verbal form from his informants at the scene, and perhaps some from brochures or other documents given on site, the student is dealing with information of different orders from different sources. He must digest all this and fuse the different modes of drama, narrative, and exposition into a whole piece of reportage. His judgments about when to quote and when to summarize what was said to him, which items and actions to describe and to recount, how to feed in explanation and general information about the enterprise, what ratio to set between visual and abstract and between human drama and information, how much of his own attitude to project—these are some of the issues the assignment is designed to raise.

First of all, the assignment requires good observation. Next, it requires some kind of note-taking, either during or right after the interview; students will have to discover a method for themselves that works best. Doing first a single interview and composed observation would prepare well for combining them here. Ideally, these papers would be balanced between information and characterization, and between firsthand and secondhand reportage. Drama, narrative, description, and exposition would be interwoven, and none used to do what another might do better for the given situation.

Some papers may never rise above miscellany, which represents a failure to find coherence either in the operation of the enterprise or in one's attitude toward it. This common difficulty usually means that the student got lost in the details and never let himself react to the totality of the enterprise. At some point in writing up the material he should survey it for general impressions and try to recall what things were salient about it. Perhaps the enterprise struck him as mechanistic, or money-grubbing, or old-fashioned, or quaintly casual, or typical of some modern trend. In other words, he could hardly not have distilled some *idea* of the operation, some essential characteristics. If he organizes around some such idea at the same time he follows chronology, he should produce a *pointed* narrative, which is by definition well on its way to being an essay. The problem of finding a good way to end the piece is then automatically solved: he strikes a note at the end—a keynote—that points up the idea or characteristic that was his dominant impression. (Calling attention to how this is done in the models should help.) Authors should have in mind a meaningful title as they are writing, one that keeps before them and the reader the unity of the paper.

Members of a workshop should tell one at a time what place they have in mind to visit. Since the product of this assignment is very closely tied to the nature of the enterprise, it's advisable, if anyone foresees difficulty with a certain enterprise, that he mention this to the author. An insurance office, for example, that offers nothing but desk and papers, is going to limit the interviewer almost entirely to the relaying of conversation. At least, the teacher and partners should know where every student plans to go and should help him think a little about the main problems in advance. Most places, however, will afford good material, and the possibilities are broad no matter where the student lives. Farms, stores, factories, hospitals, research laboratories, and transportation operations are some of the possibilities. Being allowed to choose their place usually motivates students a great deal.

Experienced students might take on more complex reportage, entailing multiple visits to the same or different sites, interviews with different people, and substantial background research in documents or other texts.

Workshop Issues

The narrative account of the visit provides a general frame, but the stipulations about conveying information and characterizing the people and the place force the student to make decisions that will modify the narrative considerably. He may interrupt it to linger over description or to inject explanation he acquired at some other point in the visit. He may digest in his own way information received from the people and feed this in gradually or in blocks, the alternative being to quote everything his informants said at just the moment they said it. Dialogue is a good way to characterize people and a readable but inefficient way of conveying information; compromise is necessary. Narrative and description will convey automatically a lot of information about the physical aspects of the people and the operation they carry on but cannot convey generalities and other unseen facts such as background, purposes, and overall method, which must come from the people through dialogue or through printed material.

Collateral Reading

The New Yorker's "Talk of the Town" sometimes includes good models for single visits, and its "Reporter-at-Large" furnishes fine examples of extended reportage based on multiple visits and interviews. But newspapers and magazines are loaded with such reportage, offered as feature articles on subjects of current interest. Also, keep around copies of reportage booklets by former students. The *Active Voices* books contain many samples covering more kinds of reportage than can be dealt with here.

Collections of news reportage are *Twentieth Century Reporting at Its Best*, edited by Louis Snyder and Richard Morris, Walt Whitman's *Civil War*, edited by Bryce Rucker, and *By-Line: Ernest Hemingway*. Books by veteran reporters cruising around with an eye out for good feature material are Steinbeck's *Travels with Charley, On the Road with Charles Kuralt*, and *Blue Highways: A Journey into America* by William Least Heat Moon. Norman Mailer, and Joan Didion have written absorbing on-assignment reportage.

Learning Other Subjects

By going as reporters to governmental, commercial, industrial, and scientific enterprises, students can gain invaluable knowledge about the workings of the world as well as about different subject areas. They learn not only what they find out themselves but what other students report in the booklets compiled from the papers. Sharing these can be a good way to help think about careers and to find out what is involved in various kinds of work. Reporting on municipal operations and state agencies will teach civics and other aspects of social studies better than a textbook ever could. For a project in science one can visit a laboratory, research center, observatory, or agricultural station. Often the reporter is given literature on site to save the breath of interviewees, and this, plus the need for more information to supplement what he sees, leads a student to extend his research into reading and to incorporate this into his final report.

Saturation Reportage

For a further development of reportage, the writer spends some extended time in a place or with a group of people not only to watch and talk but to *undergo* whatever is the chief experience of that place. An example would be going through all the procedures involved in applying for welfare, or joining fruit pickers for a day or week. *Black Like Me* recounts the experience of a white man who made himself up to pass as black and be treated as a black. Tom Wolfe's books contain many examples of living as others or mixing with others in order to report their way of life. Students reading *Hamlet* will be entertained by an example from an anthropologist, Laura Bohannan's "Shakespeare in the Bush."°

Biography: Phase

Tell what happened to someone you know during a certain period of his or her life, covering many months, perhaps even a year or so—some "phase." Refer to yourself if doing so enriches the account, but keep the focus on the other person. To be printed in a booklet. (Around 1500 words.)

This assignment returns to the earlier problem ("Autobiography: Phase") of composing material that covers a long time period. But now the material is more secondhand and therefore requires more assimilation and more inference. The author may not know the subject's thoughts and may have to infer inner life, or may have to supplement memory and acquaintance by talking with others.

It's not necessary to draw a sharp line between first-person and third-person narration, either in the student's writing or in professional writing. The narrator's reference to himself will and should vary according to the relationship between him and the subject and according to his purposes in writing about that subject. In other words, this assignment overlaps with Memoir.

Once again, the student's choice of "phase" will carry with it some central notion based on his ways of classifying experience, and this notion will naturally provide the unity of the peice. A lot of the abstracting will have preceded the writing of the paper—the assimilating and categorizing of direct experiences with the subject, actions of his witnessed, conversations with him, hearsay about him, and common knowledge of him available to the writer by virtue of moving within certain circles within a certain community.

Workshop Issues

The assignment directions are structural, rather than substantive: what a student is to write about is defined by some relationships between him and his material, not by topics. How does the writer know his subject? He knows it through three channels of information—what he saw and heard himself, what the person told him, and what was generally known about the person in the community or circles in which both moved. As informant, then, the narrator may play three roles, which we call eyewitness, confidant, and chorus. These roles give him access, respectively, to particular events, to the inner life, and to general background. The kinds of information he can convey, the point of view he can take, and the emotional closeness he feels toward his subject depend very much on which roles his actual relationship to the person permitted him to play at the time of the events. The point is that certain qualities of the memoir are determined by circumstances that limit the writer's options and must therefore become compositional issues during writing and during cross-commentary.

It follows that discussion of drafts of these papers will carry the students into an examination of their whole classifying machinery and into the sources of their knowledge about X. Papers will probably illustrate different degrees of intimacy and remoteness between the speaker and his subject. The relationship is twofold: how close were the two in real life, and how involved does the speaker show himself to be while writing the paper? A group can rank their papers in order of closeness, then determine what yardstick they were using. Do they use the same yardstick for closeness in real life as for closeness between author and subject? This leads into discussion of the author's channels of information. How does he know what he seems to know about X?

What things does he state that he could only have inferred? Are his inferences reasonable?

Some students will tell someone else's story in such a way that it's a pure account of events and one doesn't know what to make of it, why it's being told. But somewhere in the author's mind is a point, the idea of the phase, which he probably thinks is clear. Getting it to come out better may well be a factor of the author's relationship to the subject. At any rate, titling and other feedback can help the author see how to revise for the final version.

Variants

If a student were to write a biography about someone who lived in another time and place, he would have to rely entirely on documents left by others, and his composing task would be very different—and much easier, since most of the abstracting would already have been done for him. Collating source documents, weighing them against each other, and selecting from them is also an abstractive art, but it's another assignment, one that should come secondarily, and that should come easily to students who have done this one and preceding ones. The documents he would need would be those already treated in this program—letters, diaries, autobiography, and memoir plus perhaps some public records and archives. Some students might want to write a fragment of biography about a living person they do not know but might correspond with, interview others about, and do reading about.

A very important variant is the case or case history, which is a narrative about someone else who *represents* many others because of something typical in his story. A case is an instance. "Getting down to cases" means getting down to examples of a general situation. A case takes one a step beyond "Biography: Phase" in presenting the story as an instance of a generalization. In fact, students who succeed in bringing out sharply the phase that their subject went through may well have written a case, depending on whether readers can see that phase as one that some other people also go through. Cases are important in our society. A certain law case becomes a precedent referred to over and over because it represents a principle or situation. Law and business schools use cases to teach common, recurrent matters in a concrete and practical way ("the case method"). Clinical practice in counselling, social work, and psychotherapy generates large numbers of cases that become instances of one or another generalization or theory, if some expert eventually enunciates one. The key question is "What do we see in So-and-So's case that can be transferred to other people's situation?"

Case-writing externalizes, in a way that can be shared, everyone's inner efforts simply to learn from experience.

You might point out when some students' biographies amount to a kind of case, refer some students to published cases, and encourage some to write a case whether or not they have done this assignment. One eleventh-grade Exeter boy wrote about a roommate of two years before who had been required to withdraw. The result is a kind of firsthand case study, as were many of the biographical memoirs done in response to this assignment. The author was, for Exeter, a fairly average student in English, a thoughtful and sensitive person but not an especially skillful writer. The paper is presented unrevised.

THE INEVITABLE

As is the case with certain types of students, the Phillips Exeter Academy was not the right school for Albert Lockhart. All of the blame should not be placed on the school. His parents, some of his friends, and I did much to cause his failure. People too often ask, "What was the matter with Al: you should know, you were his roommate?" I usually say he just didn't try, but I know that this wasn't actually the reason.

No one can deny that this school puts a lot of pressure on the student and at the same time allows him much more freedom than most prep schools offer. Some students do well under these conditions. Al Lockhart did not.

I liked Al from the first time we met. He was about my size and was interested in nearly the same things. I was conscious of the fact that he tried to impress upon me how much he already knew about the school and how it was run. I soon learned that he was from a large city in Connecticut and that he had attended a country day school for three years. This didn't bother me too much but when he kept kidding me about not ever having had algebra I got a little aggravated.

During the first few days of school we went everywhere together. Gradually we settled down into a daily routine and seemed to separate a little. In the fall he was running cross-country and I was playing golf so we didn't usually see much of each other during the afternoons. We soon found that we had made the same friends and we usually ate with the same group.

We had many petty arguments, but prep roommates always do. Al liked the window up whereas I wanted it down, he liked

the record player turned up and I wanted it off. These were
only minor differences which we could settle by a little yelling
and swearing at each other. Compared to most of the preps who
had roommates we got along very well. But there were also
minor habits that aggravated us, little things that one doesn't
notice until forced to live with somebody over a good length of
time. Al seemed to always go out of his way to show his dislike
for certain people. There were boys in the dorm whom neither
of us cared for, but Al always tried to let it be known to everyone. He would never eat at the same table with certain people
or go into another room if there was somebody already there
whom he didn't like. At first I didn't mind this but finally it
became very annoying to have him constantly finding fault with
everybody.

There were certain subjects on which Al was pretty touchy
and I must admit I didn't ever go out of my way to prevent any
of these arguments. He was always quick to jump to the defense
of the country day school which he had attended before Exeter.
Someone would complain about how much harder it was than
their previous school. This defense became harder and harder
for him as his grades continued to drop. I used to kid him about
not going to church when he was at home. This served no purpose except to convince him that church was a waste of time.

I didn't know Al's parents especially well. From what I had
seen of his mother she seemed very nervous and talked contin-
uously while in a group. Without question she was the dominant
figure of the family. His father always reminded me of the typical football fan who never missed a game and lived only to
serve the dear old alma mater. He was quite friendly, drank a
lot, was willing to lay down his life for Yale, and followed his
wife's orders without question. I'll never forget the time Al and
his mother argued over whom he should take to a formal dance
at their club. Al wanted to take some girl he knew from a town
nearby but his mother wanted him to take another girl, a friend
of the family. After yelling at each other for several minutes
his mother held up her hand and said, "Now, Al, I know what's
best and I don't want to hear another word on the subject."
Then she walked out leaving Al nearly in tears.—Another time
over Thanksgiving Al and I were at a party with two girls. After
the party Al's father and uncle picked us up. Both of them were
nearly drunk and his uncle could barely keep the car on the
road. Al's girlfriend, who had been in a wreck less than two
months before, became very upset and told his uncle she would

rather walk if he wouldn't slow down. When we finally got back to Al's house he was in tears and so angry that he swore at his mother for nearly five minutes before going to his room. What upset me so was the way his mother took no blame for having let them come after us.

Needless to say, many of Al's problems stemmed from his parents but the school itself did much for his determent. Besides being insecure I have always felt that Al had an inferiority complex. Probably both were caused by the same things. Al didn't complain a lot but he did make many excuses for his shortcomings. He did well in his first year of cross-country and was expected to make the varsity the following year.

When grades came out for the first time, Al failed history and got several D's. He was very upset for a little while, and just sat at his desk staring at the wall. I was beginning to get worried about him but when he began to swear and slam books down I knew he was all right. I thought he would settle down the next term, and he did for a little while, but then the free afternoons the preps have became too much of a temptation. Al and Rick Cannon, the boy who lived across the hall from us, became very good friends. Rick was a very congenial guy, was quick witted, and was liked by most of the students. His one fault was that he couldn't settle down to work. I don't believe he completely finished any assignment after the fall term. Like Al, Rick had the habit of making excuses for everything that went wrong. Al and Rick would usually spend the afternoon wandering around town or watching the winter sport's teams practice.

Sometime towards the latter part of the term when things were really beginning to go bad Al started going around with Win Nickerson. Win represented the group in the school called "Negos." He spent most of his time at Van's smoking with the rest of this group and complaining about everything in general. Al had failed to make the first group in the prep sports program and this had been a letdown. His grades were very low and his attitude towards the school was rebellious.

I have always thought one of the main factors causing Al's failure was his inability to admit his own shortcomings to himself. This is why this was a bad choice of schools for him. The competition here forces a boy to know just where he stands in relation to everyone else. When he first came he was anxious to show everyone what he knew and how much he could do, just like everyone else tried. But what he couldn't accept was himself as he really was. We all have high ideals of what we think we are and at some time in our life these are shattered and we are forced to see ourselves as we really are. Al could not admit defeat or accept the fact that he was not as good as he had thought. Instead of admitting certain weaknesses and trying to improve he merely invented ways and excuses to hide his weaknesses and pretend they weren't there. He was finally forced to realize that he was only deceiving himself and then he gave up completely.

When Al became friends with Win Nickerson his career at Exeter slid rapidly. This was only a bold attempt to withdraw from the school, its pressure, and everything he was fighting. Rick Cannon had his faults but one thing he could not be accused was being a "Nego." He had a strong sense of school spirit and he disliked Win Nickerson and that group very strongly. As always, Exeter forced Al to choose between the groups he wanted to be associated with and unfortunately he chose Win.

Everyone asked what happened to Al: what caused the change from his prep year? To me there was no change. Anyone who knew him well could see what Exeter had in store for him, but instead of helping him I let things be. I'm not sure I could have prevented what happened, maybe only prolonged it, but I still failed to do my part, as did everyone else.

We see a general chronological tracing of stages in a progression, but the narrative organization is overridden by thematic organization even more than in the altar boy's autobiography. Although some paragraphs are enchained by time, most are topically related, because the author wants to score certain abstract points.

For one thing, he is seeking causes: what can explain Al's decline and dismissal? The nature of the school, family background, the boy's personality, the influence of friends he made—these are possible causes, all mentioned in the beginning and taken up one at a time later. Thus the paper is partly organized in the way many analytical and explanatory essays are—by causal factors.

Second, he wants to bring out something typical or representative in his roommate's plight. More than one previously successful, well-prepared student, accustomed to excelling in his hometown, has gone away to a selective school or college and found he had to reassess himself in the stiffer competition. Many an enthusiastic freshman has turned sour, sought escape, and started to wash out. But most recover, or at least avoid dismissal. How did Al differ from these and from the author himself? It is the representative aspect of Al's story that makes it a kind of case. In fact, this writer's interpretive account of his roommate's career resembles somewhat, even in a number of the points made, some actual cases that a faculty committee, on which I served, once wrote as part of a special study of Exeter.

The revisions this paper needs represent rather well the writing problems that workshop and cross-commentary would deal with. One concerns the channels of information. We might expect that a roommate on good terms with Al would have served as a confidant and therefore been able to relay to the reader more about what Al thought and felt during this phase of his life. But Al's inner experience is virtually absent. In such a case, the writer's colleagues should ask him about the omission. Could he include more of what Al confided to him? If Al never talked about his thoughts and feelings, shouldn't the reader be told this? Did the fact that Al kept problems to himself explain why the author was unable to help him (since the author wonders if he should blame himself)?

As for organization, it is clear that the author has some difficulty fusing the narrative and conceptual continuity, the very difficulty the teacher would expect students to run into. The paragraph beginning "Needless to say" is snarled within itself and does not lead well into the following paragraph, because the author got onto causes in describing the parents and then could find no connected way to resume chronology. Should he discuss causes along the way, only at the end, or in both places? Should such an author alternate narrative and general commentary from sentence to sentence, paragraph to paragraph, or section to section? Also, some important chronological information was lost in the shuffle between narrative and ideas. We should know, for example, just when the boy was expelled. Almost any student besides the author can point out omissions or ambiguities.

Finally, some students may want to make up a short story about something significant that happened to someone else. Help them think about whether they want to identify the narrator or not. This depends on whether the relationship is part of the story.

Collateral Reading

For the memoir type of biography in fiction, certain short stories and novels are especially worth reading, because they feature the relationship between the one telling the story and the protagonist. These novels are all memoirs of someone else who, significantly, gives the book its name: F. Scott Fitzgerald's *The Great Gatsby*, Joseph Conrad's *Lord*

Jim, Willa Cather's *My Ántonia,* Henri Alain-Fournier's *The Wanderer,* and Robert Penn Warren's *All the King's Men.* Typical such short stories are John Steinbeck's "Johnny Bear,"* Guy de Maupassant's "Mademoiselle Pearl,"* Sondra Spratt's "Hoods I Have Known," and Herman Melville's "Bartleby, the Scrivener."

Most biographies are based on research rather than memory. Titles are too numerous to mention. As with autobiographical books, it's better to let students choose the person to read about. Or they can start with an interest in space travel, medicine, car racing, rock or soul music, nuclear physics, and so on and look for a biography of someone in that field. Many students will learn a lot of specialized or even technical information from reading about someone's life who would not yet read a book on the subject itself. Plutarch's *Lives of the Noble Greeks and Romans* and John F. Kennedy's *Profiles in Courage* contain short biographies that are not memoirs. In her *Common Reader,* Virginia Woolf wrote vitas, such as "Mary Wollstonecraft,"° of important feminine figures. Benjamin Quarles's "The Abduction of the 'Planter',"° exemplifies some biography in minority literature. Obituaries are an interesting sort of biography, and students should be aware of biographies in encyclopedias.

Robert Coles' *Children in Crisis* and his other books in that series provide excellent examples of cases. Robert Lindner's *The Fifty Minute Hour* is a very readable book of psychiatric cases.

A very large number of short stories are made-up cases, since the purpose of most fiction is to show something about life through characters designed to typify people of a certain age, stage, class, temperament, situation, background, and so on. Willa Cather's "Paul's Case" is just more explicitly titled. (Conrad Aiken's "Silent Snow, Secret Snow" is a similar case.) Sherwood Anderson's *Winesburg, Ohio* and James Joyce's *Dubliners* may be regarded as the fiction writer's casebooks.

Reading simultaneously in biography, fiction, and cases drawn from medicine and psychology and social work will sensitize students to rhetorical differences between clinical or specialized, general, and artistic stories or cases.

Chronicle

Write a narrative about a developing trend or situation that took place in a large group or community that you know about. To print in a booklet. (1200 words.)

"Chronicle" is defined as group narrative. The material of chronicles may stem from three sources—memory, special visits and interviews, or documents and records including photos. This assignment shifts the subject from the third person singular to the third person plural and thus broadens it from an individual to a group experience. This shift automatically makes the subject more abstract, since the author must see something common in the behavior or activities of a number of individuals. In other words, he is concerned only with some action that shows one aspect of a number of people; they are trying to raise funds for schools, ostracizing some other people, vandalizing for entertainment. Counterparts of this assignment are cases about groups, fragments of local history, and communal short stories such as Shirley Jackson's "The Lottery." A "group" could be anything from a large bloc of townspeople to a clique within the school. The assignment should be framed so that students do not leap yet from what *happened* to what *happens*; this is a generalized narrative but not a generalization. The classification of behavior that underlies the student's story may be a very simple one based on physical action, but he is very likely to classify also the motives or traits behind this action. This amount of generalizing is a natural concomitant of the assignment and will often provide the point of the account or be a conclusion of it.

Workshop Issues

Technically, this assignment poses the problem of recounting events that may not be sharp incidents that happened at such and such time and place but relatively vague occurrences, diffused over time and space. For example: "The antifluoridation faction launched a violent counterattack." To make such "an event" vivid or specific the student will have to illustrate by recounting one thing they did on a certain occasion, just as he might give examples of any other kind of generalization. Ideally, he should find some balance between sentences such as this, which state the historical fact, and more detailed references to the smaller incidents of which it is an abstraction. Ordinarily these references would come as follow-up sentences of the first, which would lead the paragraph. The paragraphs would presumably follow in chronological order, since this is a narrative assignment.

But what about summary of background information? Should this be placed in a block at the beginning of the paper, or fed in along the way? It's a matter of judgment that should be discussed when individual papers are read. *Must* the information be placed first? Does it make the opening so slow that the reader loses interest at the start? What if the first paragraph were narrative—began with an incident—and the block of information came after the reader was "hooked"?

Workshops can perhaps most help an author by considering his draft in relation to the sources of his material, since sources determine many compositional choices. A group might, in fact, talk over their material *while* doing the draft. Memories, notes on interview-visits, and other people's documents and records create different constraints and possibilities. Should an author add a source he does not yet have?

The eleventh-grade boy who wrote the following group memoir was having a hard time not only in English but in other subjects as well. He was a good athlete and a hard-working student, but his academic background was weak by Exeter standards, and he was intellectually undeveloped when he arrived the year before.

EVEN WITHIN THE LINES

My neighborhood is a typical middle class Negro neighborhood. The homeowners try to make sure it looks as nice and neat as possible. All the homes are worth between $18,000 and $25,000. Most of the homeowners are well educated, most of them being school teachers. By 1957 our block was completely filled except for three lots. One was next to our house. It was quite narrow, so narrow that it looked as if it might be part of our lawn. Across from it were two lots owned by old Mrs. Hathcock, who planned to will them to her two sons.

In the summer of 1957 the lot next to our house was bought by Mr. Gray and he announced plans to build on it. Although several people were skeptical about his plans, no one refused to sign the petition he had to present before he could get city water and start laying the foundation for his house. The house went up very quickly, and the time taken to build it was an indication of its value. It had been made mostly of used lumber taken from demolished homes and it was much too large for the lot. It was wooden and white, which made it unique in the neighborhood. All the other homes were made of dark brick and are set far back on their lots. Mr. Gray's white wooden house stood about five yards from the sidewalk and was worth about $8,000 or $9,000. It was completely out of place in the neighborhood. When our neighbors realized what was being built, they raised a great uproar. But it was too late to do anything about the situation. They would just have to wait and see what Mr. Gray made of his property.

Everything went fine that first year, although the house was out of place, no one could complain about the way My Gray kept it looking. It was as neat looking and well kept as any of the other homes, if not more so. By the first part of 1959 it began to show a little wear. That winter Mr. Gray caught pneumonia and was hospitalized for several months. By the time he was able to resume taking care of his house, it was in very bad shape; the wind had been very tough and had taken off part of his roof and a great deal of his siding, and the old wood used in the house had become infested with termites. The more the house deteriorated the more restless his neighbors became. They were not interested in his problem. They were only concerned with the value of their property, which was decreasing along with the deterioration of Mr. Gray's property.

By the late fall Mr. Gray was desperate. He had done the best he could to keep the property value up, but he had neither the funds nor the health to do it successfully. He had a new problem. It seemed that the petition he had had passed when he had first built his house had been registered in the wrong office, and he had to obtain a new one. He needed to have at least twenty-five names on the petition; he was only able to get six. He was beaten when his neighbor on the other side. Mr. Wilson, offered to buy his property for a low price. He had no choice —he had to take it.

Just before winter hit, Mr. Wilson had the house torn down and the foundation filled. Now again our block is a straight row of dark brick houses and there are three vacant lots on it.

It's interesting to know that man's inhumanity to man doesn't cease, even within color lines.

The four middle paragraphs all start with time expressions, indicating the narrative order, but each paragraph contains statements about the growing alarm and antipathy of Mr. Gray's neighbors. The first paragraph starts in the present tense of generalization, then shifts to the past tense for the transition into narrative. The last paragraph returns to the present tense of generalization but asserts a more abstract statement, philosophical rather than expository. The author created this structure by treating the needs of the subject, not by following teacher advice or corrections, though his experience with previous narrative assignments surely helped him a great deal to see what he should do.

The only indication of the first person is "our," but the account could only be told by a local inhabitant, a member of a "chorus." The subject is more impersonal because it is plural. The author has no "confidant" information; the inner experience is the collective reaction of the whole neighborhood to an intruder. Had he known Mr. Gray well, however, and known his mind, the story might have been very different—a biographical fragment. So the paper is chronicle partly because of the point of view the writer *had* to take: he knew only what everyone in the community knew; he was only a member of a chorus (though a dissident member).

Collateral Reading

In addition to the reading suggestions implied earlier, the students might bring in magazine articles that chronicle recent trends among certain groups or in a certain town. Popular disaster stories are chronicles. Though large-scale history can be very dry, because overcondensed, close-ups of historical moments can read like top adventure stories. *American Heritage* and *Journal of Negro History* are a couple of periodicals that publish short pieces of history. Maurice Herzog's *Annapurna* and Bruce Bliven's *The Story of D Day* are examples of whole books that chronicle a suspenseful event in detail. *Time of Torment: nineteen sixty-one to nineteen sixty-seven* by I. F. Stone and *My Lai Massacre and Its Cover-up: Beyond the Reach of Law?* by Joseph Goldstein et al. exemplify modern chronicles told to raise serious moral issues.

Chronicles include case histories. Berton Rouché's *Eleven Blue Men* and *Other Narratives of Medical Detection* are chronicles that might be considered as cases. *Points of Departure* contains four cases that shade off into profiles and two chronicles that shade off into two short histories.

Short stories: Bret Harte's "The Outcasts of Poker Flat," Edgar Allan Poe's "The Masque of the Red Death," and Stephen Crane's "The Open Boat." Novels: Ray Bradbury's *The Martian Chronicles*, the J. R. R. Tolkien trilogy, Albert Camus' *The Plague*, Jean Merrill's *The Pushcart War*, Sheila Burnford's *The Incredible Journey*, and William Golding's *Lord of the Flies*. Reading chronicle fiction may inspire some youngsters to do their own. It lends itself to adventure and science fiction, among other possibilities.

The following four briefly stated assignments support the strand of fictional narrative by providing launching places for made-up stories other than points of view. Sometimes students need to focus on a type of subject matter, as in the first two, sometimes on a form inherited from tradition, like the latter two. All points of entrance that work are good, and part of individualizing is to provide a variety of them. Students choosing one of these four will not forget what they have learned in point-of-view assignments when they write and discuss papers done from other departure points. Most youngsters will tend to tell these four kinds in third-person and thus make them fictional biography and chronicle, but those grown more sophisticated from experience writing in this program may think to do the first two from some first-person points of view.

Science Fiction. Imagine that one important aspect of life as we know it has changed—such as a lower global temperature or an imbalance of a certain chemical or plant life or a new ability to read each other's thoughts—and tell some events that would follow from this new condition. You might tell this as a group story, featuring some representative people, or as one or two people in particular experience the events. To get ideas, ask, "What if . . . ?" Read some science fiction—and some science. A good factual basis makes the made-up parts more interesting. You might get partners to write stories following the same major change and talk over first what indeed the real facts are that you're going to have changed.

Sports, Adventure, Mystery Stories. Take some intriguing newspaper account of events and imagine a whole story around it featuring sports, adventure, or mystery. A family crashed in their private plane during a storm in the mountains and some are still missing. Look for such story ideas as you read or hear some bare or incomplete facts. What else happened, before or afterwards? What was the real cause of what happened, if it is not clear from the account? Make up more details about what kind of person or people did what was reported. Add other characters and events that seem needed to extend the account. Or focus on a setting or a scene or an event or an arresting person that you recall or have heard about and imagine a story featuring the place, scene, event, or person. Tell first to get things a bit formed in your mind, then write and share that way too.

Legend. Take some person who really lived and whom you admire and tell his or her feats on a grand scale, bigger than life, to bring out the strength or quality you admire. Feel free to invent, but start with the main truth of the person's accomplishments. You might think of another situation or force for him or her to apply the strength or quality to. Or think first of a major problem or danger our world faces, then imagine a hero or heroine who can conquer it and tell the exploits by which he or she does this. You and partners might choose the same problem or danger. Read some legends to get the feel, and consider doing yours as a poem or ballad.

Myth. Make up a fantastic story as a way of explaining something you find puzzling, awesome, or hard to believe—phenomena in nature or yourself or people's behavior. Read some myths. Some tell how the world was created, some "explain" earthquakes or lightning, and others tell how such and such an animal got its spots or horns or bobbed tail. Create with partners a whole mythology or set of linked myths in which the same characters and places and objects recur. One explanation can in this way relate to other explanations so that all help to make sense of each other and form a complete picture (cosmology).

The following three assignments comprise a progression parallel to the series "Narrative Illustrating a Generality" to "Generalization Supported by Instances," which follow. That is, they too bridge between narrative and generalization by a shift from instance to idea. But these three—parable, fable, and proverb (or saying)—represent folk fiction and its characteristic way of expressing general truth through story and metaphor.

Parable

Read some parables and invent a story of about 400–800 words that makes a general point about people but does not state the point. Draw material from either our current world or remote or imaginary times.

A parable does not linger over details or get involved in a complicated or extended plot. It does, however, make its point in an entertaining way by embodying it in story form and by letting the reader draw the conclusion. The parable form really aims at generalization but avoids explicitness in favor of an incident or events that constitute, in effect, an instance of what the generalization would be if it were stated. This requires considerable control of the material, because if the narrative is not pointed enough, different readers will conclude different things, which is not the purpose of such a folk form. It exists to impart a clear piece of wisdom in a pleasurable way. Whereas many other sorts of folk tales spin elaborate chains of events and embroider these in rich detail, the setting and situation of parables are quickly established, and nothing is told that is not telling. Some students might get ideas for parables from newspaper stories or incidents that happen around them. Sometimes it may be easier to allegorize with remote or imaginary materials, which are not already so loaded with implications as everyday reality is. In any case, reading instances of the form is critical for picking up both its purpose and its technique.

Workshop Issues

Since the main issue, besides just telling a good story, is making the point come through implicitly, this is a fine place to title each other's papers without knowing the author's title and then discuss the group's titles for each paper. This should help greatly to show authors how well the point came through or, if not, what changes they might make. See "Narrative Illustrating a Generality" for more.

Collateral Reading

Every folk literature has its parables, so that collecting them becomes a way of representing different ethnic literatures. First, of course, are Christ's in the Bible. The books of Idres Shah contain many fine Sufi parables, and Paul Reps includes some of the wonderful Zen parables in *Zen Flesh, Zen Bones.* They may usually be found among the works of folklorists like Maria Leach or Harold Courlander, who has gathered some from Africa. Authors like Leo Tolstoi and Robert Louis Stevenson wrote parables.

Fable

After reading several examples of fables, write one of your own by telling a very brief story that makes a moral point or observation about life. State the moral in a separate sentence after the story.

The fable joins parable to proverb by comprising both story and statement. It catches narrative at the precise moment that a generalization is explicitly distilled from it. So perhaps better than any other form of discourse it represents the bare relation between *instance* and *idea.* La Fontaine said the fable is the body; the moral, the soul.

La Fontaine also said, of the use of animals, "You begin by seeing man through animals and end up seeing the animal through men." It was he too, however, who pointed out that even Aesop did not always stick to animals and that fabulists certainly have not since. Students should feel free to make plants, objects, and people the material of their fables, but animals have an unquestionable appeal up to a late age and help to make fables popular with the young.

A mini-curriculum can be built around the fable. To appreciate the full value of students writing fables, consider this cluster of activities:

- Write a new version or modernization of a traditional fable, perhaps in a very different style.
- Read a fable without the moral; then write a moral for it and compare with the original moral.
- Take a moral from a fable and write a new fable to precede it.
- Take a proverb or other generalization and write a fable to illustrate it. Test by having a classmate write a moral for your new fable and compare this moral with the original one.
- Turn a parable into a fable by thinking of a moral that seems to fit it.
- Convert a fable into a poem.
- Find a fable that was not intended as such, in a newspaper or magazine item, and write a moral for it. Post together.
- With a few other students write different fables for the same moral and post or print these together.
- Test a fable by taking off the moral, reading the fable to other people, then asking them what moral they would give it.
- Discuss whether a certain fable and its moral are in fact true.
- Perform a fable as a small group, devising a way to render the moral differently from the tale (by a chorus of "witnesses," for example).
- Make a class collection of fables and print it up.

The compactness of fables makes for a comfortably short reading and writing length but still yields substantial content for discussing, acting out, or rewriting. Even more than parable, fable provides a model of lean narrative; everything builds toward the point, and nothing is mentioned that does not help. Students who learn well to crystallize a story into a statement are doing what is required for writing a "Thematic Collection of Incidents," where each brief narrative must show the same point, and will also be ready for that classic coordination of illustration with generalization that is the heart of most explicit idea writing. As a fine bonus, fables are often done as poetry.

Collateral Reading

As with parables, we can make the reading of fables an occasion for sampling literature of other cultures and ages. It, too, is a genre that individual authors have taken over from oral folk literature. See *Aesop's Fables* (Illustrated Junior Library edition, Grosset and Dunlap, 1947); *The Fables of La Fontaine* by poet Marianne Moore (Viking Press, 1954); *Black Folktales*, Julius Lester (Richard W. Baron Publishing Co., 1969); *Fables in Slang*, George Ade (Dover Publications); *Fables for Our Time*, James Thurber. Since many collections of folk tales from other cultures will contain fables, parables, and proverbs or sayings in mixture with each other and other literature, you can look for all at once.

It's better for students to define the fable, and other forms, from reading and working with a number of instances than for a textbook or the teacher to define for them. Starting with someone else's definition short-circuits a student's thinking. Though not an advocate of "model writing" in the specific and sometimes tediously analytical way many teachers practice it, still I'm clearly proposing in this program that students read in the kinds of discourse they are writing. When they are writing in a particular literary form inherited from tradition, a generous sampling of others' previous efforts is downright necessary. Inductive defining makes the novice do his own analysis—which allows him not only to take in and take over the form but to use it more fully and expressively.

Workshop Issues

Keeping all detail to the point and matching tale to moral are the chief issues. Some students may find that they really *want* to elaborate a story more for its own sake than for the sake of a moral. Peers should be taught to spot that and to put the matter positively: "It looks to me like you might have to sacrifice too much to make a fable out of this story. You could finish this one the way it's going and just think of another story for a fable." Even professional writers start out to write one thing and finish with another. We don't want someone who has chosen a fable but not yet achieved enough control, or has gotten diverted to something perhaps equally good, to feel he has failed or not obeyed some rules. Individual choice should exist partly to help people shift themselves into the right assignment, which means they will sometimes overshoot or undershoot, but finding out what one is doing and what one can do is the main aim. The writer can again choose— whether to revise for better coordination with a moral or to write something else than a fable *at that moment*. Test the relevance of details by experimentally removing them to see if partners and author feel it makes a difference in setting up the moral.

Test the fit between tale and moral by leaving off the moral, as well perhaps as title, until workshop members have written what they think the moral (and title) might be. Adjusting a moral to climax and conclude a fable affords excellent practice in precise, thoughtful wording and constructing of a single sentence. The tense shifts from the past to the present tense of generalization. Now the writer faces economy of another kind. He has to state in one catchily turned sentence what the story part was about (extract the theme, if you like). This task will cause some students to overload the sentence and spoil the fun—and perhaps the point too. Others may fashion an arresting moral but one that does not truly distill the events, at least not in the view of others. Here working with fables raises a real-life issue: people frequently draw different conclusions from witnessing or experiencing the same events. So adjusting the fit between moral and tale involves us in broader and fascinating matters characteristic of all composition: people see things differently but have to share views in order to understand each other. Youngsters will, like adults, come up with different morals for the same stories. This is a good problem that workshop discussion of fables can help students work out. As they try to show each other where they differ in interpretation, where they feel conflict between the story and the statement, where changes can be made to resolve differences, they'll be learning both how to compose better and how to discover inevitable discrepancies in viewpoints.

Proverb and Saying

Read some proverbs and sayings, then write a number of your own, using a comparison or figure of speech to express some (when a good one occurs to you), and expressing others as a regular generalization. Each stands alone as a separate sentence that can be made into a poster, button, T-shirt, bumper sticker, or page of a calendar or can be collected into a booklet with others.

A proverb or saying is a total discourse complete in one sentence. It takes several variant modes of expression that are themselves instructive to work with. A proverb makes its statement of generalization through a metaphor: "A rolling stone gathers no moss." An epigram employs wit or elegance—some paradox, antithesis, other rhetorical device, or original turn of phrase: "Work is the curse of the drinking class" (Oscar Wilde). Adage, aphorism, epigram, and maxim are all statements of general truths or sentiments varying mostly in emphasis on being commonplace (adage), terse (aphorism), elegant or witty (epigram), or a guide for conduct (maxim). But these all overlap a bit. "It's a wise child that knows its own father" could be any except a proverb. So the best policy seems to be to lump them together except to distinguish between figurative (proverbs) and literal (all others, or sayings).

A youngster of virtually any age can formulate a generalization in only one sentence (growth being toward the ability to sustain and develop one throughout a longer discourse, for which this assignment will prepare). Proverbs may seem more primitive but are in fact often harder to understand and to write than literal sayings, because readers may interpret them in more than one way and writers have to devise an original metaphor. But content and diction influence difficulty also, of course. At any rate, proverbs in particular offer an excellent occasion to focus on metaphor organically, that is, without trumping up motiveless comparisons or doing vivisections on poems. Similarly, sayings in general allow us to focus on the sentence without stripping it of context. (The only context, by the way, is the reader's experience, which must fill in the generalization, supply it with instances or illustrations, and ultimately ratify or reject it.)

There's no problem about what to do with student proverbs and sayings. Along with those culled from books and word of mouth, and along with morals from fables and even scientific or philosophical generalizations, we can:

- Choose one and discuss the truth of it in a small group. Make it part of the discussion to try to think of instances of it, evidence that would prove it, and ways of revising it that would make it more acceptable if it seems not true enough (qualify, quantify, rephrase, etc.).
- Choose one as a topic for an essay ("Generalization Supported by Instances").
- Find or make pictures to illustrate some. (This separates figurative from literal, because "Birds of a feather flock together" cannot merely be illustrated by a flock of birds. The illustrator has to deal with the fact that a proverb can be applied to potentially many situations because it's a metaphor.) Illustrate a collection of sayings, perhaps including proverbs. Use to make posters, displays, calendars, stickers, and buttons.
- Write a fable that will conclude with one as the moral.
- Look for single sentences in books or periodicals that can stand alone as a proverb or saying. Post on a sayings board or collect as a booklet. Cite sources.
- Select two or three that seem to be true and seem to be addressing the same subject well enough to try to combine as a syllogism. If they are true, what new generalization logically follows? This can be done as a group discussion or by an individual working up an essay topic for writing "Theory."

Collateral Reading

There are many whole books of proverbs and sayings. See, for example, *Proverbs of Many Nations,* ed. Emery Kelen; *Book of English Proverbs*, V. H. Collins; *Dictionary of American Proverbs*, David Plotkin; *Proverbs and Common Sayings from the Chinese*, A. H. Smith; and *Wit and Wisdom from West Africa*, Sir Richard Francis Burton. Some writers have given special attention to epigrams, like Ambrose Bierce, who did his as entries in *The Devil's Dictionary*, reminding us that definitions may take the form of epigram. Older poets often did epigrams as one-sentence poems. Benjamin Franklin put his, of course, into *Poor Richard's Almanac*. See also La Rochefoucauld's *Maxims* and Pascal's *Pensées*. Many sentences in literature have stood out so arrestingly that they have become detached from their context and quoted as if they had been written as sayings, like couplets from Alexander Pope or William Blake or the many entries in *Bartlett's Familiar Quotations*.

As a lead into such books, and to give students an eye and ear for good one-liners, start a proverbs-and-sayings board by posting up ones you've gleaned, including some plucked from current newspapers and magazines. Encourage students to add to and cycle the sayings and to make separate posters for sayings they have found or written. It can become a class passion. Today's sayings are found more in the environment than in books, and the environment is one of the best places to look for them and also to place one's own.

Workshop Issues

Many practices for the workshop have already been implied. Whether students are going to post or print their sayings, or use them as topics for discussing and writing, I would emphasize *tinkering* with them, trying out changes in wording, phrasing, sentence structure, imagery, and sound, to adjust statements for greater validity and to make their sayings wittier or terser or more gripping. Take advantage, in other words, of this blow-up of the sentence to develop diction, syntax, metaphor, and style. Workshop members can write revisions of each other's saying that the author can take or leave. Or revising can occur as members discuss the offerings.

Directions

Write step-by-step directions to a particular audience for how to do some action such as play a game or operate a machine,

*or for how to make something. Say what the activity or product
is supposed to be, and tell everything a person needs to know
to do that, including which materials if any. Your directions
will go to your audience to carry out and can become part of a
how-to-do-it book.*

Most directions take a chronological order, for at least a goodly part
of the way, because they direct someone through a sequence of acts.
And yet a set of directions often must describe materials or situations,
as well as explain reasons or relationships. Directions constitute, then,
another transition between narrative and exposition. They differ from
narrative in not being set in the past, of course, but time order nevertheless makes for a very similar organization. Directions differ from
all the other assignments in another significant way: they include the
imperative mode as well as the declarative. Compare this assignment
with "Narrative Illustrating a Generality" and "Fable": the three offer
variant ways of arriving at discourse of generalization through narrative or time order.

Any student knows how to do or make *something*. It's easy to find
material and motivation for this assignment. In fact, students in classes
where this assignment has been done were eager to read each other's
directions, both to learn to do what others can do and to find out what
others know how to do. Directions are to carry out. They are kin to
scripts, since both exist to be performed, like blueprints. This orien-
tation toward action makes this kind of writing especially sensible to
students who may not yet see many other reasons to write, especially
in this do-it-yourself era when people are trying to return to an earlier
self-reliance as the penalties for dependence become greater and more
obvious.

Directions offer a good occasion to practice coordinating prose with
graphics, since illustrations often make the directions easier and
clearer. What can words do better and what can pictures do better?
This is a crucial issue. Many illustrations may need labels or captions.
Some directions must be affixed to an object or machine as operating
instructions and so constitute a kind of environmental writing that
teaches the coordination of writing with things themselves rather than
with pictures only.

Directions are hard to write. Try it. They challenge our precision of
expression but more than that our clear-headedness and our objectivity. Classic misdirections fail to allow for the viewpoint of others not
as familiar with a subject as the author and thus smoke out in an
especially effective way that central bugaboo of all writing—egocentricity. Think, for example, just of travelling directions. Though still

allowing youngsters to organize mostly by the familiar order of time, directions really constitute expository writing and should be regarded by teachers as affording practice of a sort that will pay off for other expository writing.

Collateral Reading

The best ideas for how-to reading will come to you from just browsing through the average well-stocked magazine stand or book store. *Popular Mechanics* was an early leader, but now you can find printed matter on how to do or make things in virtually any area of interest from car repair and gardening to getting scholarships and controlling your brain waves. The appeal is enormous to kids, who want to become independent and are drawn toward new-age trends in alternative-energy devices and processes or simply toward ways of surviving during hard times. Booklets from the Government Printing Office, agency brochures, articles in newspapers and general magazines are other sources besides how-to books and periodicals on special subjects. Have students bring in everything they can find and place on a how-to shelf along with the booklets they make. The best single source of titles is no doubt Stewart Brand's *The Next Whole Earth Catalog,* which refers to them under topical headings.

We should remind students that directions include not only recipes but some verses and songs like jumprope jingles and game songs and the square dance "caller's" lyrics. Reading directions in verse or song will inspire students to try their hand. Also, some direction-writing is only a joke or fancy and provides a stimulating form in which to express whimsy or emotion. See, for example, the poem "How to Paint a Perfect Christmas" by Miroslav Holub.

Workshop Issues

The nature of directions puts workshop exchanges on a very practical basis. To ensure greater success in writing, some students might try out directions orally on workshop members to work out some of the bugs and have a clearer idea of how to set up their directions. Frequently, for example, it's hard to know when to bring into the main line of directions a sub-set of directions or ancillary information, but listeners can discuss this with the author before he goes to paper. Then paper drafts can also be "field-tested" by having some of the target population try to follow them. Sometimes the author can be present and see for himself where readers go awry, as, for example, after writing paper-folding directions for younger children.

A very interesting procedure, which I have seen done with fifth-graders, consists of group members making something at the same time they're writing down the best way to say what they're doing (making puppets, for example). They discuss and revise the directions directly from their experience as they go along.

However obtained, feedback can be brought back to the workshop, where partners can help find ways to improve known trouble spots. Sometimes more accurate or specialized vocabulary is needed to name and refer to things more clearly. Sometimes the order of directions should be changed. Sometimes more background or explanatory information needs to be fed in. But, again, so often the writer assumes too much and does not realize what he's omitting that a reader needs to know or how a certain cumulative effect leads the reader other than where he intended. Workshop members can bring more objectivity to bear on this issue than the author can alone, and indeed this is a main purpose of collaborative revision.

The following five briefly described assignments would especially accommodate less-developed children in approaching the more formidable assignments to follow. They represent easier ways of writing discourse that does not rely on time order, of dealing with facts and ideas.

Labels and Captions. Write labels for objects around the room, articles in an exhibit, or cut-out or original pictures. (This develops naming and phrasing—nominals—along with sensory acuteness.) Write captions of a sentence or paragraph for your own drawings, one at a time at first, then for linked series to tell a story or explain something. Do the same for photos or cut-out pictures. Post up, pass around, or affix to display. Labels and captions can be serious and accurate, even technical, or humorous and ironic or whimsical. Include labeled and captioned pictures, charts, graphs, maps, and other illustrations in your reportage, research, or other factual writing.

Homemade Encyclopedia. Alone or with partners, make an encyclopedia about a special subject you know much about or want to know more about. List all the items you can that need to be described and explained and write an entry about each one. Ask about sources of information. If you are a group, decide on who will do which entries. Illustrate if appropriate and if you can. Explain it to the whole class then place it where classmates can look at it and refer to it. Print up and distribute if possible.

Wishes. Describe in detail something you would like to do or be or have happen to you. (This makes a kind of essay.) Take the subject from something you daydream a lot about; give it full expression so you can see the full extent of what you want and perhaps why you want it. Illustrations? Share with few or many, depending. . . .

Editorial. Write your opinion about something, saying perhaps what has made you conclude this and giving evidence or arguments you think will persuade who you are writing for. Who *are* you writing for? Think of some outlet for your views as you write—a newspaper or magazine ("Letters to the Editor," perhaps) or some flier you can distribute by hand or by mail, or some special place for posting statements of opinion.

Speech. Write what you would like to say to a particular audience. You might really deliver this talk to it later. If that is not possible, write it as if you could and plan to deliver to the class or to print it in a mock newspaper as if it had been transcribed from your delivery. You might want to inform or warn or persuade or ask something of this audience. This might involve illustrating or backing up your points according to what it takes to get across to your audience.

Narrative Illustrating a Generality

> *Narrate any true happening or experience that illustrates a point you want to make of a general nature. In other words, you are telling a story not only for its own sake but also to show something that the reader could apply to people and events he knows of. This can be in first or third person. To print in a booklet. (800-1000 words.)*

The purpose of this assignment is to ensure that students learn to connect incident and idea, to make narrative function in the service of a generalization. Essentially, this narrative should be just one long illustration of an idea. As such, it prepares directly for the next two assignments, which gradually reverse the ratio between incident and idea until the idea dominates and the narrative element is distinctly subordinated. This purpose certainly overlaps with that of "Parable," but it's important to offer students a fictional and traditional form as well as this more open assignment based on actuality. "Parable" differs also in its succinctness and moral tone.

The best way to get this assignment across is through examples of the results, which may be drawn from booklets of these papers made by former students and from features, columns, and certain other departments in newspapers and magazines.

Workshop Issues

To fulfill this assignment well the student must bend all the elements of the story toward the generality, especially if the generality is to be left unstated. Group discussion should develop and apply the criteria for assessing these papers. Is the generality clear? Responders can write on a slip of paper what they think the generality in paper X was, if it was not stated explicitly, then read these slips aloud to see if they agree. If not, the problem would seem to be that the author has classified the action in a more private way than he thought and failed to see that others might take the action as an illustration of some other idea. This may be so, but the problem might also be that he has not controlled details well enough, that he digressed just enough here and there to mislead the reader about what was significant and what was not. This is analogous to the position of someone giving directions how to get somewhere who forgets how many *irrelevant* streets and intersections his listener is going to encounter that will look like the ones he's describing. On the other hand, it's very satisfying to the student to learn from the returns that his audience got the point without his having to spell it out.

To be safe, of course, a student could always make a direct, abstract assertion of his generality and repeat it fore and aft just for insurance. But another criterion should be that the writer not be heavy-handed by explaining too much or spoiling the reader's pleasure in discovering the point. It takes very sound perspective and objectivity to know when the nature of the events will communicate the generality to the reader and when the author must make the point explicitly—but this is just the kind of judgment the student should develop. Putting oneself in the reader's shoes is the key to more than one writing problem. Sometimes the title alone will make clear what otherwise would be ambiguous; often a light touch at the end will do it. Finally, one criterion is bound to be the worth of the generality. One cannot help valuing more the narrative that points to a less recognized truth than one that draws a shopworn conclusion.

Collateral Reading

A large proportion of writing classified as "essays" is actually narrative of this sort, such as George Orwell's "Shooting an Elephant." This is the place to read a number of such essays. Much pointed journalism of the "feature" sort fits this assignment, not deadline news but news reflected on and told for its timely generality, not just for its newsworthiness. You and the students can compile anthologies of these. Newspaper columnists often generalize from an incident, as exemplified by Jon Carroll's "Chair Chat"° and Ellen Goodman's "A gift to remember."°

Thematic Collection of Incidents

Tell briefly several different incidents that seem to you to have something in common, that are joined in your mind by some theme or idea. You may draw these incidents both from your personal knowledge and from your reading. State the theme only as much as you think you need to. To print in a booklet. (1000 words.)

This is a crucial kind of composition, because it weans the student from organization by chronology to some other organization. He can follow a time order only when he is telling one of the incidents; since the next incident will be a new beginning, he must bridge by means of the idea. Doing this assignment entails collecting several items that are similar in some way and putting them under the same heading, the items in this case being the incidents. Chronologic will not hold them together; some other logic must. The logic invoked is some logic of classes. If the incidents are summarized in a pointed enough way, so that the similarity among them is apparent, and if the author's classification is objective enough, the paper should be a successful one, at least logically.

Regard the wording of this assignment just as a description of what the writer does, not as how to put it to students. From trials with both youngsters and teachers it's clear that this way of casting the assignment makes it seem very difficult or odd when it's not. The problem is that the departure point or stimulus to write this kind of essay lies elsewhere, in the writer's effort to show something he has observed across several experiences occurring in different times and places, or in dawning feelings of similarity, a sense of a theme or motif that keeps cropping up. However you cast the assignment, you will probably have to illustrate it immediately with samples. Call this an article or essay, and draw examples from newspapers and magazines. They can be obvious or mind-stretching. A simple example: someone notices that a customer in a grocery store prefers no-deposit-no-return bottles to recycled ones; that the street near a litter barrel is littered; that a recent proposition for preserving public land has been voted down; and that a poll just taken shows that more citizens are antagonized by having to pay for auto smog devices than approve of them. This person concludes that the public does not want to protect the environment enough to make minor sacrifices for it.

The fact is, however, that despite the extreme commonness of this sort of writing, students may not produce it as readily from this assignment as from trying to do other kinds of assignments such as "Diary Summary" or some form of reportage or memoir. The main thing is to sponsor kinds of writing that will make it happen at one time or another, and to know how to help it along when it does occur, because collecting incidents around a theme, synthesizing them into a generality, is basic to thinking and so makes a fine kind of essay. The physical model for this assignment would occur if you spread on a table a miscellaneous collection of objects and asked someone to sort them into piles. We are constantly sorting the happenings we see or read about into classes. Most kinds of expository writing are based on classifications, often public or traditional ones. When we do our own thinking we do not always know what classification we are assigning to our experiences and so we often do not communicate clearly about them. Take what follows here, then, as guidelines for working with such writing when it occurs. Or try to get it to occur by simply having directions say to write another piece like some samples, and have a generous and interesting collection of samples from other students' writing and from periodicals.

In order to illustrate the process most clearly I have chosen as an example a very successful paper written by an eleventh-grade boy in a class of mine at Exeter.

NOISE IS A TOLL OF THE DEVIL, OR QUIETNESS IS NEXT TO GODLINESS

It's well before eight; the tremendous hall is absolutely vacant; the students haven't started filling it yet. I'm on a bench way off in a corner, quiet because I'm occupied with watching and recording what goes on. Someone comes up the stairs towards chapel, snapping his fingers in the emptiness of the hallway. He comes through an entrance, still snapping his fingers and whistling between his teeth softly and tunelessly. He sits down, and as the squeak of the bench fades into deep silence, he gazes uneasily about, then begins pounding out a rhythm on the bench and on his hymnal. This sustains him until some friends come slowly in; he calls to them, then converses.

In church Sunday the guest minister sits back, then at the end of the sermon hymn, gets up and goes to the podium. For

a long minute and a half he stands there looking down, saying nothing. The congregation shifts uneasily in seats, wondering "What's the matter? Doesn't he knew he's supposed to start talking? Doesn't he have a sermon prepared?" At last someone coughs, then many others. A whispering starts, each boy turning to his neighbor and discussing the situation. The time draws to a close, and the minister explains that the silence was calculated to produce a reaction, as it did, of uneasy noise.

Uncle Screwtape, a shade high in the hierarchy of hell, writes to his nephew Wormwood, whom he has been advising on Wormwood's work on his patient on earth. "Music and silence," he says, "How I detest them both! How thankful we should be that ever since our Father entered Hell . . . no square inch of infernal space and no moment of infernal time has been surrendered to either of those abominable forces, but all has been occupied by Noise—Noise, the grand dynamism, the audible expression of all that is exultant, ruthless, and virile. Noise which alone defends us from silly qualms, despairing scruples, and impossible desires . . . The melodies and silences of Heaven will be shouted down in the end!"

In Orwell's 1984 there is a gathering of all the adults in an area to a hate meeting—where established symbols of their hate are flashed on the screen, and the people looking at these symbols shout and rant and threaten and become bleating sheep. A chant rises from the group, a chant in which everyone participates with fervor, helplessly, and screams at the images. After a long time, they are lulled and leave, united and feeling fulfilled after their experiences together, better citizens for their society.

A few nights ago I had a tremendous amount of things to do—I was despondent and worried. From across the hall there was coming a large volume of sound—a record player blasting out surf guitar music, and eight guys shouting and laughing, two on the floor wrestling. For a few desperate minutes I sat at my desk trying to work, banging my fist on the desk and kicking the wall. Then, my always low power of concentration snapped, and I went in to join the fun. It was deafening, but I got so wrapped up and produced so much sound myself that I passed an hour, admittedly a carefree one, without even thinking of my work.

With all these examples I'm not trying to preach and show everyone how their time should be spent—singing celestial anthems or sitting in silent meditation. But I do always notice,

when I'm asked to bow my head in silent prayer, how my thoughts wander frantically until they fasten on something I can day-dream easily about. I notice how embarrassing any silence is, and I wonder how long I could sit in an empty church and keep my mind free from earthly thoughts. I know how infectious noise is at a football game, and I've seen films of crowds watching Hitler and caught up in the chant. Noise is attractive, as Screwtape says, because it is distracting. Silence is embarrasing because there is no protection against oneself, no barrier that prevents trespassing into realms of forbidden soul-searching.

Workshop Issues

For many students, narrative is a kind of haven which they are reluctant to leave because chains of events have a ready-made organization, whereas exposition requires that the student create and assert a new order that is not a given of the material. This assignment is transitional: the order in which the student places the several incidents may not be important, but they must all illustrate the same theme and he must find some way of getting from one incident to the next. Group discussion of the first or final drafts should continue to test an author's classification against the perspective of others. Further: Is there one incident that does not fit the theme or classification as well as the others do? Are some of the incidents summarized in such a way that their relevance is not clear? Does the order of the incidents make any difference? Would the paper be more effective if they were placed in another order? Does the author make transitions between incidents? If not, does he need transitions? If so, could they stand without transition? (Would juxtaposition alone make the point?) Does the author state the main idea in the title or in a sentence or paragraph? Where does the statement come—at the outset, at the end, or during transitions? Sometimes withholding the statement until the end creates a suspense and permits the reader to make up the classification along the way. He may even have to change his classification midway as he encounters new incidents—and this could be very thought-provoking. But if the connections among incidents are too hard to make without guidance, then the author should have made his statement early in the paper or used the transitions to guide the reader. Some discussion about how well the examples from real life and the examples from reading go together might be profitable also.

A student who masters this assignment should have no trouble with that classic problem of coordinating example and statement, of illustrating generalizations. Examples are always drawn from a level of abstraction lower than that of the statement being illustrated. Frequently the examples are narrative. The difficulties are (1) summarizing the bit of narrative so that it will fit under a heading containing other bits of summarized narrative, and (2) finding an apt and accurate heading that can logically contain the examples assigned to it. (Note the similarity with a fable, though a fable has only one example.) The narrative summaries must be trimmed of irrelevance and worded abstractly enough to stand clearly as one item sharing similarities with other items in its class. This is precisely what is required when illustrating generalizations in a piece of exposition.

A variation of this assignment is to have the student draw *all* the incidents from recent reading selections, possibly mixing poems, plays, and fiction. This could amount to an essay test, and it may well tell the teacher more about what the student has been getting out of the course reading than a teacher-chosen topic. Most topics that are at all specific carry built-in classifications so that essentially all the student has to do is find examples from the reading that fit the teacher's classifications. Naturally, the student does less thinking in this situation than the teacher and, furthermore, gets no practice in *creating* classifications, which he must learn to do. Nor does he get a chance to test his classifications against other people's. When students do tie together the reading in their own way, the papers usually are more interesting than when they have to write on an assigned topic. Also, assigned topics invite students to dope out the idiosyncracies and views of the teacher and to give him what they think he wants—a tendency that leads to much artificial and dishonest writing.

Another possible variation, if a student has written a lot of narratives, and has done the earlier assignments in this program, is to draw all the incidents from his past writing. The advantage of doing so is that students can then understand as they never would any other way how the raw material of life is processed by stages into more and more inclusive generalizations.

Generalization Supported by Instances

Make a general statement about some aspect of people's behavior that from your own observations seems true to you. Use a number of examples to illustrate your generalization. Draw your examples from among the things you have observed and read

*about that led you to this generalization in the first place.
(800–1000 words.)*

This assignment calls for the classic article or essay most encountered in professional writing and most sought by teachers of writing in schools and colleges. It covers the "essay questions" of examinations, most "term papers," and the kernel structure of most of the world's expository writing not covered by the following assignment. This is so because the assignment makes the very process of inductive reasoning itself the structure of the discourse. But I trust it's quite clear that assignments in this program have been about ideas from the very first. What really distinguishes this assignment is not that it deals with generalization but that a generalization governs the organization, the chaining of statements and of paragraphs, so that some other logic than chrono-logic determines the structure.

Working with "Proverb and Saying" would be an excellent precursor to this assignment. Having generalizations of their own at hand, and having practiced fine-tuning a generalization till it fits what one believes, will stand students in good stead here.

Limiting the subject to people's behavior is, of course, not at all necessary but makes a good starting point because everybody knows something about this large, accessible body of material. A variant of the assignment is to generalize about phenomena in the rest of nature. Inasmuch as generalization is the tense for stating laws, and inasmuch as the inductive process is the heart of the scientific method, this assignment logically accommodates scientific writing. Whether the subject is people or other marks the division between the social and physical sciences. Whether formal or informal is a matter of style and rhetoric.

A teacher who would like to use this assignment as a means of getting students to write about the reading could simply ask them to draw all their illustrations from the reading selections in question. This would prepare for common essay questions found on college exams.

Workshop Issues

A generalization should be a statement cast into the present tense. But generalizations may be of different degrees of abstractness, depending on how much time and space is covered by the statement. If the paper contains no past tenses, this means that the illustrations are also generalizations, though presumably of a lower order than the main statement. The question, then, is whether such illustrations *illustrate* well enough or whether they themselves are so abstract as to require examples. In other words, each paper will embrace a certain segment of the abstraction hierarchy; the highest point will be the main assertion and the lowest point will be the most concrete example. If the main assertion is high, such as "Men have a strong need for exploration and adventure," one would expect the secondary assertions and the illustrations to run high also, though they should still be well below the main assertion. But if the main assertion is something like "Older sisters are more confident than younger sisters"—a much more specific generalization—one would expect all the other statements in the paper not only to run below this one but to dip down into past-tense, narrative sentences, which are near the bottom of the hierarchy.

To make useful comments on the papers, it helps to have a strong sense of levels of abstraction. "Concrete" and "abstract," "specific" and "general" are entirely *relative* to the master statement that provides the context for the whole paper. Illustrating is translating a statement down the hierarchy. What is a generalization in one paper might be an illustration in another. But if the illustration is not very much farther down, it cannot illustrate well. If it is too far down, it may be too trivial, relatively, to be persuasive ("My friend so-and-so joined the Peace Corps last year because he was restless" to illustrate "Men have a strong need for exploration and adventure"). Rules such as "Be specific" and "Don't overgeneralize" are meaningless and unhelpful. The student must play up and down the abstraction ladder according to the situation, jumping down for limited cases of the generalization, jumping farther down for illustrations, and then jumping back up occasionally for transitions or other restatements of the main idea.

"Overgeneralizing" is not a matter of making too abstract a statement, which can never be wrong in itself. It is a matter of *failing to qualify* the statement, failing to tailor it to fit the truth exactly—using *if, some, usually, whenever*, and any number of other words and clauses that limit the time, place, number, conditions, etc., in regard to which the generalization is true. It's natural and often very productive for workshop members to discuss the truth of each other's generalization, but it's very much to the compositional point not merely to argue over a statement as it was first written but to discuss how it might be altered to meet objections to it. This will naturally involve students in sentence modification and exploration of syntactic resources.

Illustrations should be distinctly subordinated, and paragraphing should follow a logic inherent in the generalization. Although the task calls essentially just for an assertion and examples, most generalizations break down in some way into lesser ideas or into variations of the main statement. Thus, a typical pattern would be for the first paragraph to assert the generalization and for the lead sentences of the following paragraphs to make the substatements, with follow-up sentences illustrating them. But, of course, there should be no formula for such a paper. The first paragraph might consist of an arresting example that is to be explained later, or the substatements might lead inductively up to the generalization as the conclusion of the paper.

Some common faults are: letting an illustration run away into irrelevance (usually a narrative for its own sake); piling on examples that all show the same point; stringing the examples with weak transitions such as "Another example is. . ."; repeating the first paragraph as the last paragraph; and repeating the main generalization instead of developing it. Almost all of these faults stem from too simple a generalization. Developing the main statement through qualification and variation would solve most of them. But bear in mind that this assignment does not invite a logical step-by-step development, and that illustrating a generalization naturally tends toward a string-of-beads organization. The best papers, however, will find a way of stringing them artfully and with as much development as the subject accommodates.

An eleventh-grade student of mine at Exeter wrote the following.

CHEATERS

Some of the golfers cheat all of the time, and all of the golfers cheat some of the time. That is an axiom that usually holds true. In the five years that I have been playing the game, I doubt if I've met an honest golfer. I don't care how scrupulous a man is in his daily life; put him on the golf course, and I guarantee his golfing companions will corrupt him.

Not all golfers cheat with the same regularity, nor do they employ the same methods. For example, the seventy shooter could not use the crude methods to which the duffer, striving to break 100, must resort. Nor would the duffer profit by using only the more refined techniques of the par shooter.

As my golfing companions represent various degrees of skill, a description of their methods of deception should include most of the deceitful practices seen on the golf course.

Mick is the best of my golfing partners. He usually shoots around par and occasionally breaks it. For a golfer of Mick's caliber, the opportunities for cheating are few and far between. As he usually takes only four or five strokes per hole, he cannot rely on poor memory to reduce his score. If he is to cut even a single stroke, he must employ the most subtle techniques.

One of Mick's favorite tricks involves a shot hit out of bounds or a lost ball. The penalty in each case is two strokes. Mick rarely loses a ball, but often another member of his party will. When this happens, Mick will say, "Toss another ball out in the fairway. You'll be lying two, hitting three" (assuming that the ball was lost on the tee shot.) Mick knows the rules of golf, and he's fully aware that the boy is actually lying three, hitting four. Mick gives him this break because he expects the same treatment should he hit an errant shot. In the club house when Mick is bragging about breaking par, his opponent cannot bring up that forgotten stroke, as he was guilty of the same sin.

Mick, also, is able to gain an occasional stroke through use of the "double putt." Any putt of three feet or less he deftly backhands in. If he misses, he says, "Guess I'd better putt that one. Thus, he gives himself two chances to make the short putt.

Most golfers who play regularly score somewhere between eighty and one hundred. Tom is a good representative of this class of average golfers. When it comes to cheating he employs the same methods as Mick, but is also able to make use of a few others. Occasionally Tom will have a disastrous hole. If this hole is any worse than a triple bogey, you can bet that arithmetical error will eliminate at least one stroke.

The best way to distinguish the average golfer from the expert is that the average player rarely plays the ball as it lies. Tom, for example, always plays winter rules (winter rules allow the golfer to give himself a preferred lie by moving the ball with his club-head for a distance of no more than six inches). Tom not only uses these rules in mid-summer, but also frequently improves his lie when in the rough. This is something winter rules strictly forbid.

Mike is the member of our foursome who represents the biggest class of golfers—the duffers. For him each round is a frantic struggle to break 100, usually ending in dismal failure. Mike has been playing for over five years but still has not mastered the fundamentals of the game. However, when it comes to cheating, Mike is a pro.

One of his favorite techniques is pencil pushing. This can be employed only by the scorekeeper, and Mike is quick to volunteer to undertake this task. The pencil pusher simply reduces his score a stroke or two before marking it on the card. I would estimate Mike plays five to ten strokes better when he is keeping score than when he is not.

Mike is a master of the foot mashie. This shot is used chiefly when the ball is behind a tree or in a bad lie in the rough. It is of special advantage because it is never recorded on the scorecard. The shot consists of a light glancing blow by the side of the foot, which causes the ball to roll a short distance and out of trouble.

When a greater distance is to be covered, Mike finds the "pitch and run" effective. This should not be confused with another shot of the same name often used around the greens. Mike's pitch and run resembles the foot mashie in that it is never counted on the scorecard. The shot is especially effective when Mike finds himself in deep rough, and none of his playing partners are looking. He simply picks up the ball and, with a flick of the wrist, tosses it ten to twenty yards nearer the fairway. This is usually enough to give him a clear shot; if not, a couple foot mashies can be applied.

Cheating in golf is not limited to casual play. In my hometown, the city tournament is played under winter rules. One reporter, covering the tournament, recorded over twenty violations in which a player had given himself a preferred lie while in the rough.

A story I read a couple years ago in "Golf Digest" is the classic example of cheating. It involves two men, Sam and Joe, who were playing a match for the rather high stakes of ten dollars a hole. On the first hole Sam banged a 250 yard drive down the middle of the fairway. Joe sliced his tee shot into the trees and thick rough on the right. Previously, they had agreed to take only ten minutes in hunting for lost balls. At the end of the allotted time, Sam said, "I'll go ahead and play out the hole. If you find your ball before I finish, go ahead and play it. If you don't, you'll have to forfeit the hole." Sam hit his second shot into the middle of the green and was lining up his birdie putt when Joe's ball came plopping down two feet from the pin. Sam missed his putt and lost the hole to Joe's birdie. Completely unnerved, Sam dropped the next three holes. Who could blame him for being upset. After all, he had Joe's ball in his pocket.

The only group of golfers who play the game entirely honestly are the professionals. Of course, these men cannot afford to have their reputations ruined by dishonesty, but it is deeper than that. For these men, golf is a livelihood, and they have great respect for the game. Just as the banker, businessman, or lawyer is honest with his clients, so is the professional golfer with his scorecard. I have heard of several instances in which a professional has accidentally touched his ball, moving it not

more than a fraction of an inch. No one saw this, yet the golfer reported it and added an additional stroke.

All this points out a basic facet of human nature. People rarely cheat in things which they regard especially important, such as earning a living; however in relatively minor things dishonesty is rampant.

One can see here the overlaying of one organization upon another. The larger one is based on development. The author moves from good golfers to average ones to duffers; then he shifts from amateur play to tournament to professional contest, the last of which allows him to end with a new version of his generalization—that cheating at golf is a particular case of the broader truth that people cheat at play, not at work. The significance of this order—the fact that shuffling the sequence of topics would make a great difference—is what we mean by "developing an idea."

Within each category of golfer the order of examples is not significant: whether pencil-pushing or foot-mashie comes first makes no difference except for ease of transition between them. Thus the string-of-beads organization is embedded within a meaningful progression. But in many papers it will be dominant, perhaps because the subject truly provides no development, perhaps not. Cross-commentary can help determine which is true.

Collateral Reading

Generalizations on contemporary issues and other matters abound in periodicals such as *Commentary, The Black Scholar, The New York Times Magazine, The Rican Journal, Harper's*, and the *Atlantic*. Many good reading selections may be culled from columns, reviews, editorials, transcripts of speeches, and books of essays. Classic essayists are Michel de Montaigne (who coined the term), Jonathan Swift, Charles Lamb, William Hazlitt, Thomas De Quincey, Ralph Waldo Emerson, Henry David Thoreau, George Orwell, Virginia Woolf, Joan Didion and Alice Walker. As personal essays, examples are Loren Eiseley's "The Hidden Teacher"° and Annie Dillard's "Seeing,"° as formal thesis, "Whiteness"° by Herman Melville and "The Functions of War"° by Leonard C. Lewin. Generalization articles can be found for every field or discipline in specialized journals. Alexander Pope's "Essay on Man" illustrates generalization written as poetry.

Research

Pick a subject you want to know more about that you cannot get well enough informed about from observing and interviewing—something that requires investigating books, files, records, and other documents as well. Go to these sources, take notes, pull all the information together around whatever question you're trying to answer or issue you want to explore, then write this up as a set of generalizations that state what you've found and that are supported by facts and ideas from your sources. Write this for an audience that you envision as having a certain amount of interest and background regarding the subject. Print and distribute to this audience, or submit for publication to an appropriate periodical.

All fact-finding is research. What is meant by it here is getting information from documents, photos, films, tapes—any *stored* information. If observing and interviewing are useful in addition, that's fine, of course, but the emphasis is on documents, most of which are of the sort included in this program. Exceptions are public records, files, archives, and material in other media.

Almost all book research that students are asked to do in school and college is on subjects assigned to them, the main purpose being either to force students to "cover" certain material staked out in a course or to elicit evidence that they have done the required reading. This serves institutional purposes better than it teaches true research. Canned research does not entail the same intellectual work as making up one's own thesis from materials one has to seek out oneself. Furthermore, since this kind of work is demanding and presupposes very strong motivation, it's crucial to let the student choose his subject according to what he really wants to know about. The best way to teach research is to put it on the same realistic basis as the professionals do. They get on the track of something and pursue it through whatever sources they can find.

A group of less-experienced students might first do this assignment as a team, different individuals going to different sources after determining together what they want to find out and where the sources are. Some members might do observing and interviewing while those more ready for book research could divide up documents. Later they bring together what they've found and talk out how to proceed from there. From the rub-off effect, those not ready for research in documents will learn something of how to go about it—what standard references and indexes are in libraries, how libraries are organized, how to find out what books and articles have been written on a certain subject, which periodicals specialize in certain subjects, what documents are not found in libraries but elsewhere in municipal or state records, what other institutions or agencies, like museums or unions, might have relevant information, how to get at newspaper files, what other media, like computerized data, offer by way of stored information, and so on. Naturally, you and other adults can help this knowledge to enter into a class and make its way around as individuals acquire it and pass it on. Gradually, more and more individuals become savvy about the techniques and can appreciate *why* one should bother, when they see interesting and really informative products issue that classmates and former students have done. By role-playing adult professionals, students will do some impressive, original research that the local historical or archaeological society, newspaper, Lions Club, community center, or whatever may well want to publish or at least read or hear.

See encyclopedias for an assignment that might precede this one in earlier years.

Workshop Issues

Assuming that individuals benefiting from a prior group project have written a draft of their research article, they can now respond to each other's papers, first, by sizing up what they're aiming at and checking out whether authors are taking advantage of relevant sources. Authors should bring notes and other material with them and let each other see literally where they're coming from. Of course, if members described before what they were trying to do and what sources they intended to go to, it will be possible now to assess how well they have succeeded in finding and summarizing what they wanted to know. Often authors will have good reason to redefine their project in the light of what they found out and what responders say about it. Generalizations that once seemed to do justice to the data may have to be reformulated. The group can help with this and spot holes in the information or matters that need more explanation. It should remind authors to use charts, graphs, other graphics, and other media when feasible. Generally, it isn't necessary to have a strong notion in advance of what a workshop should do for these papers. Compositional issues we have raised for other expository assignments will often apply here—where the relation between data and generalities fitting the data only gives a slightly new wrinkle to the instance-idea relation. Besides these, the problems of research tend to be of a practical, sometimes mundane sort that just good will and good collaboration can solve.

Traditionally, teachers have made heavy weather out of the format for reporting book research, especially for footnoting and assembling a bibliography. This superficial form, which looks very scholarly (and can easily be taught as rote information) doesn't touch on the real procedures of research mentioned above or the composition problems. Professionals simply consult the style sheet of the publisher to whom they are submitting a manuscript, because publishers vary in how they want citations set up. Citing is a very mechanical matter, for which no single procedure is correct, and should not be made to appear as an important aspect of research. Direct students to *some* style sheet as a guide (that of the Modern Language Association is as good as any), say that citing is traditional and necessary information for the reader, but take the mystique out of it and don't let them get hypnotized by it at the expense of the research matters that really are hard.

Collateral Reading

Make a list for students or get them to compile a list with you of periodicals that routinely or frequently report research that they can understand or care about. Some fields, like history, rely, of course, more on documents than some other disciplines, but even experimental science has previous research as its context. Work out a way of keeping and making available copies of students' research papers and other booklets that might interest later students like those in *Active Voices*. Build up a classroom library of student work for browsing, to furnish models of assignments, and to inspire successive generations. Many of the reading selections previously recommended for other assignments will serve here too, since biography, chronicle, and some reportage entail recourse to documents. See "Malta"° by Elizabeth Pepper and John Wilcock, "Mullein"° by Michael Moore, and "Myth"° by Mircea Eliade.

Theory

Take a generalization such as your main statement in a previous paper and combine it with two or more generalizations of the same sort so as to develop a theory. The subject of the theory should be something that you know a lot about from personal observation and from your reading. Illustrate with examples and argue with proof. Your conclusion should be a further statement that is not evident in any of the original statements. To be printed (1200–1500 words.)

Whereas the latter assignments were based on the logic of class inclusion and exclusion—classifications—this assignment is based on the logic of propositions—the combining of separate generalizations by logical connections. What was the main point of generalization assignments is the point of departure here: the student must assume several generalizations as premises. Writing this paper entails some kind of syllogism or other way of combining statements. If proposition one is true and proposition two is true, then such and such new proposition is true. The various possible ways by which one proposition or generalization can be related to another is the proper subject of logic, and this is indeed the place to undertake practice of logic. But an abstract survey of the possibilities in advance is not likely to remain with the students or to be very readily applied by them. The best method, again, is to launch the students into this assignment and let them examine the results afterwards.

The importance of having the student argue a theory about a subject he really knows is to prevent him from borrowing arguments he has heard or read, for in that case the paper will be merely an elaborate kind of copying and there is little chance for him to learn from it. An excellent point of departure, if this is possible, would be for the student to take generalizations he created in "Proverb and Saying," "Narrative Illustrating a Generality," or other assignments, reflect on some of their ramifications, and combine them to see if new statements can reasonably ensue. Ideally, all the propositions he manipulates in this paper would have been drawn from his previous papers. He would then be forging an entire thought structure of his own. But failing this, students can still do their own thinking by taking generalizations from each other or from books and combining these with their own and in their own way. If one thinks such-and-such and so-and-so is true, then it follows that he must think certain deductions from this are true too. Good preparation for this assignment would be for a group to write on a chalkboard or easel several generalizations they accept as true and to try combining them to see if they can also accept the implications of their all being true. If not, why not?

Workshop Issues

Because of the difficulty of this assignment, it would be good to let group members work with each other's papers at several stages along the way by talking about ideas before writing and by talking out ideas further after a first draft. What are an author's starting generalizations, and how does he combine them? What does he conclude? Suppose, for example, his propositions are:

Conformity is a process of growing up.

Conformity is the essence of society.

Conformity is dangerous.

Some of the common connectives, of course, are conjunction, opposition, and cause-and-effect. Whereas the logic of classes depends on analogy—sorting according to similarities—the logic of propositions depends on tautology—the setting up of verbal equations showing that one proposition is equivalent to another proposition. This is done by transforming the first proposition by means of a series of logical operations, syllogistically. After showing that X is another way of saying Y, the author is then able to plug generalizations into each other so as to develop a theory.

Of course, the logic of propositions is founded on the logic of classes, but the classifications are liable to be hidden. So much is assumed that definition becomes a complicated problem. It's not solved, however, by beginning every theory with a quotation from the dictionary. Dictionary definitions assume previous dictionary definitions so that the student is apt to get caught in a verbal circle. If he can foresee that his reader will not know in which sense he is using certain key words, then he should say early in the paper what meanings he is giving to these key words.

A good procedure for experienced students is to raise their hands at any point in the reading of a paper when they do not understand a statement or do not understand how one statement follows from another. During the ensuing discussion of the problem, they should try to ascertain whether the difficulty lies in the syllogistic relating of the *propositions* or in the logic of the underlying *classes*. Can they pluck out the starting generalization and the derived one(s) and test them out as a syllogism? What is the logical skeleton of the paper? Is there a hidden proposition which has not been referred to so far in the paper? Would a better definition of one of the key words clear up the matter? Would something that is not explained until later be better explained at this earlier point? Also, they should try to distinguish between the validity of the premises and the validity of the manipulation of the propositions.

On the rhetorical side, the author might choose to state his conclusion in the first paragraph and then go on to prove it, or to suspend his conclusion as a climax to the paper. The group should discuss which of these alternatives seems best for the given paper. If the argument is difficult and subtle enough, it may be necessary to state the conclusion at the outset. And again, what is determining the author's paragraphs and the order of the paragraphs? And, of course, we must still ask if the illustrations fit the statements. In addition, has the author illustrated the statements that need most to be illustrated?

This example by an eleventh-grade student of mine at Exeter illustrates some of those issues.

A STUDY OF CONFORMITY

It is often assumed that people consciously conform. This is seldom true. Conformity is either a process of maturing, or a subconscious development. In either case, it is the essence of society.

Conformity as a process of growing up occurs generally at an early age. For a small child it is natural to try to emulate grown-ups. The child attempts to speak as they speak, walk as they walk, and act as they act. Children often pretend to be grown-ups because of the natural desire to conform to the adult world.

This force decreases as age increases. It disappears simultaneously with the "loss of innocence." When a child, or even a teen-ager is exposed to derision or disillusion, his dream world crumbles. This, however, is often a gradual process. The natural instinct to conform, therefore, gradually fades away as the child becomes more and more exposed to the world.

It is very hard to say when loss of innocence occurs. Certainly, vestiges of it carry on well into the teens in many people. This may seem incredible, but it is true. The average senior high school American History textbook is still concerned with Alvin York single-handedly winning World War I and George Washington chopping down the cherry tree. The United States is always moral, always right. This unreality shows the extent that even high school seniors are protected from unpleasant truths.

When the illusionary world of innocence is destroyed, a replacement must be made. These replacements come in many different forms. Charlie Gray in *Point of No Return* finds himself in an artificial world of conformity. He dresses like everyone else, works in a bank like everyone else, rides the right train and belongs to the right country club. Many will say that Charlie must conform in order to keep his job. This is not entirely the case. Conformity is a replacement for his lost naivete, a means of keeping himself from falling apart. Only by conforming to his artificial world can he tolerate it.

Conformity at Exeter is obvious. The greatest objection to it, however, is the form is takes. To adults, the sight of a bored, lazy, apathetic boy is repelling. To them it seems a waste of what should be a happy, exciting time of life.

What these adults fail to understand is why the "innocent scared little prep" becomes a nego. The answer is glaring. If a prep comes to Exeter scared and innocent, his situation is soon exploited by his fellow students. He is baited beyond his ability to tolerate abuse. His self-respect and innocent values are destroyed. To attain any sort of security, these values must be replaced.

At Exeter there is only one possible replacement—negoism. To protect himself from being baited a boy must assume an air of indifference. If he shows that he is hurt, the smell of blood will make the sharks all the more vicious. But this is not enough. To prevent being baited a boy also has to destroy his individuality.

Superficially, most Exonians are the same. Their dress, general vocabulary and actions are almost identical. Even their values are the same. High school is great, Exeter is bad, parents and faculty are not reasonable or human, the Dean is a sadist, sports cars and liquor are good, and finally the purpose of life is the fulfillment of animal desires.

This behavior is condemned by the adult world. To them, conformity to the extent of loss of individuality is wrong. The paradox of the situation is never observed. It is the adults who have to belong to the right country club.

There is a rule in chemistry called Le Chatelier's principle. In essence it states that when a stress is applied to a system in equilibrium, the system must adjust to counteract the stress. This is also very applicable in explaining human behavior. The world of the innocent is a system in equilibrium. When an outside force upsets the system, it is the system itself that must change. Whether or not the system changes to life in a grey-flannel suit or negoism is immaterial.

This argument should not be taken to mean that a person willfully and consciously conforms. That is ridiculous. No person can be objective enough in examining himself to be able to state exactly what steps he should take in order to become more popular, or less vulnerable to baiting. Similarly, nobody can control his actions sufficiently to truly fit the image he has set for himself.

Instead, conformity is a sub-conscious attempt to gain security. It is an adjustment to the demands of society. For most people, it is a natural reaction. Because of this, there are very few non-conformists in the world.

Due to the variance in the extent of the stress on different people, conformity comes in varying degrees. In cases of great stress, there exists a case of over-conformity. Over-conformity is a concept, not a scientifically defined segment of behavior. The symptoms of over-conformity are easily detectable. Artificiality of emotion, behavior and speech are the most apparent signs of the disease. Others such as inability to think independently are also prevalent.

It is customary for many writers and thinkers to repudiate over-conformity. *Point of No Return* is such a repudiation. Many of Sinclair Lewis' works reflect this too. In fact, the whole expatriate culture of the 1920's was against the over-conformity of American society.

Over-conformity is not attacked for the sake of attacking it. It is the result of over-conformity which is repelling. At Exeter the natural tendency is for a student to write a "nego"-style theme. This is not because the student really wants to write about Exeter negoism—most students try to avoid it. The intellectual sterility of the Exeter climate is so great, however, that this form of expression completely dominates the style of student writing.

Conformity is an inevitable product of society. To oppose it is to defy the universe. This does not mean, however, that conformity can not be controlled. Indeed, it is vital to the interests of society that conformity be restrained.

The danger of conformity is intolerance, as intolerance leads to a stagnant society. For society to be fruitful, intolerance must be suppressed. Conformity must be allowed only as long as it is tolerant. Unfortunately, this distinction is very difficult to make.

In the past, conformity has followed a cycle. A mode of behavior and expression is accepted, and gradually becomes the model for society, to the exclusion of all others. The society soon ceases to become intellectually productive. A small group of individuals will revolt, but for a long time society does not tolerate them. Eventually, tolerance does increase until the new order replaces the old. This order, in turn, wears out to be replaced by another.

This cycle explains the various literary, musical and artistic movements of Western Civilization. To us, looking back, the cycle seems the best way of keeping our culture fresh. This does not mean, however, that society recognizes that the cycle is necessary in the future for the continuation of our civilization.

Many people dislike "modern art," "modern music," or "modern writing." They can not understand how it can be meaningful expression. They support the changes of the past, recognizing them as a vital part of our heritage. Furthermore, they know that at the beginning many of these movements were not tolerated. But at the same time, they oppose any future change. Intolerance is typical of society.

I predict that within twenty years, the styles of expression that are beginning to be accepted now will become a materialized movement, very possibly past its prime. It, in return, will be gradually replaced. The present movement, like all others, will appear well-defined with recognized advantages and disadvantages. When it is worn out, the advantages growing thin and the disadvantages becoming more evident, a new movement will be started as a reaction to the accepted style. When this happens, there again will be people who want to freeze progress.

Conformity is a paradox in itself. It is recognized as inevitable, yet it is never accepted. It is based on intolerance, and at the same time its very intolerance is both criticized and praised. It is a function of the complexity of society—the more complex the society the greater the demands of conformity.

Without conformity our civilization would have no foundation. Yet without non-conformity we would still be in the stone ages. Perhaps our complex, contradictory system of conformity is the only workable form of progressive civilization[12]

The three generalizations about conformity that we presented earlier as examples were, of course, drawn from this paper, and the reader can see for himself which conclusion the boy drew and where he placed it in relation to the premises. Workshop commentary would probably have helped him to improve the continuity in some places and also the balance among illustrations.

The frame of the paper is syllogistic, multipropositional, but this boy quite spontaneously embeds within this frame several orders of dis-

---

[12] One of Exeter's main contributions to the intellectual growth of its students is in permitting them to write about its "intellectual sterility."

course of lower abstraction levels, through which he has already worked in previous papers. That is, after announcing two of his premises in the first paragraph, he narrows down to one in the second paragraph—that conformity is a material part of growing up. For a long sequence of following paragraphs, he proceeds to substantiate and develop that generalization exactly as if he were only doing the preceding paper in this sequence, paragraphs three and four dealing with substatements about conformity as a process of growing up, and the other paragraphs in the sequence dipping down nearly to the narrative level for the instance of Charlie Gray, and then back up slightly for the more generalized (and digressive) example of Exeter behavior. Then he surfaces later for his third premise—that conformity is dangerous—without signaling it very well, and launches into another documented generalization that lasts nearly to the end and contains the digressive example of art vogues. The second premise—that conformity is the essence of society—is treated in undocumented and scattered fashion, reappearing in connection with the conclusion. For such a difficult kind of composition, however, this student has done very well, especially without group help with the kind of difficulties that one would expect to encounter with this assignment.

Collateral Reading

It's in the nature of theory and of higher thinking in general that it occurs in a particular field, not as a form unto itself, so finding appropriate reading selections is a matter of looking in fields of interest. Charles Darwin's *The Origin of Species* argues a theory on the basis of zoological information. Ruth Benedict's *Patterns of Culture*, Claude Lévi-Strauss's *The Savage Mind*, Marshall McLuhan's *Understanding Media*, Karl Marx' *Capital*, Kate Millett's *Sexual Politics*, Michael Polanyi's *Personal Knowledge*, and Alan Watts' *Psychotherapy East and West* are well-known, available books that emphasize theory. Some articles or self-contained chapters consist of a theory or hypothesis, like Karen Horney's "The Dread of Woman"° and John Michell's "The Serpent Power."°

Additional Poems

Let's end now with assignments for some more poems. Repeatedly, we have pointed out how various assignments in all three groups might be done as poems, but here are a few that require other departure points like traditional forms or music or just very personal associations and fancy. If I have not dealt with poetry separately, it's because poetry extends over the whole range of these progressions—and then some.

Songs

Write new words to a familiar tune. Just try out different words until some begin to fit that make some kind of sense or nonsense, then follow whatever that idea is until you have a new set of words. (Lewis Carroll did this in *Alice in Wonderland* to make fun of old songs or poems.) Teach your song to others. Agree with some partners on a tune, then each do new words and compare and make a booklet giving the original tune.

Make up your own song, both music and words. Start with either a tune or a nice line or so of words. (Songs make a good way into writing poetry because melody sets up a metrical pattern of feet and stresses and phrasing in a non-mechanical way.) You might practice by trying to set to music a poem you like, or write a poem to fit a tune you like. Next—do a musical . . . perhaps with partners! Perform, make a tape, make a booklet.

Limericks

Every true limerick has exactly the same form—same number of syllables stressed in the same places, so that it's possible to test one by singing it to a limerick tune. The form itself acts as a stimulus. Read and listen to some limericks then write some of your own. Just play with the rhythm and meter and let the words come out zany. Make booklets of limericks with partners and record funny renditions of them, using sometimes more than one voice per limerick. Or just post on a limericks bulletin board. To perfect, try out on partners and ask for suggestions.

Picture Poems

Focus on some image or picture that sticks with you and begs to be put into words. It may be a memory or something you see every day, but somehow it gets you inside. Put it into words—not many perhaps, just a few well-chosen ones. Make use of comparison, rhythm, and word sounds, where to break the ends of lines, the tone of words. Write a poem, in other words. Try it out on someone or several people, then play with it some more, until you think it gets the picture—and your feelings about it—across. Post on a poem board, set to a tune, illustrate, include in a booklet, or send to a newspaper or magazine.

Haiku

Catch in three short lines, perhaps one sentence, a moment, an act or feeling or image that will be gone in another moment. What glimpse, sound, smell, taste, touch has ever triggered a strong, sudden feeling? Read some translations of haiku to get the feel, and notice what devices and effects they have. Try your hand and share in any ways you can think of.

There are other forms of poetry you might want to try writing in— some new, like cinquains, and some, like villanelles and rondeaus, quite old.

Occasion Poems

There are a million ideas for poems if we think of their being written to fill a function on a particular occasion. Imagine a poem that is

a lullaby	advice
a farewell	an invocation (calling on some force or personage)
a will	a speech
a blues	a eulogy (statement of praise)
a greeting	a sermon
an epitaph (headstone verse)	a dialogue
an elegy or dirge (funeral lament)	a response to a news item
a blessing, or benediction	an insult
a curse, or malediction	an invitation
	a prayer
a direction or recipe	a mantra (to repeat to oneself to keep the mind in a good place)
a blow-by-blow sports-cast	a celebration
a suicide note	a confession
a bread-and-butter letter	
a catalogue (listing)	
a prophecy	

Casting a poem as one of these makes it no less poetic but provides a particular purpose (often fictional) to stir and guide imagination. It adds a dramatic context in which a kind of character voice speaks. Many might, therefore, be excellent for performing and recording as well as for printing up in mixture or by category.

COLLATERAL READING
FOR STUDENTS

Here are the contents of the anthologies of professional and student writing referred to in this book. The professional selections in the two anthologies following are suitable for some secondary students.

Points of View: An Anthology of Short Stories

Edited by James Moffett and Kenneth R. McElheny
(Penguin USA, 1966)

Contents

Interior Monologue
But the One on the Right, *Dorothy Parker*
This Is My Living Room, *Tom McAfee*

Dramatic Monologue
The Lady's Maid, *Katherine Mansfield*
Travel Is So Broadening, *Sinclair Lewis*

Letter Narration
A Novel in Nine Letters, *Fyodor Dostoevski*
Jupiter Doke, Brigadier General, *Ambrose Bierce*
A Bundle of Letters, *Henry James*

Diary Narration
Flowers for Algernon, *Daniel Keyes*
The Diary of a Madman, *Nikolai Gogol*

Subjective Narration
My Side of the Matter, *Truman Capote*
Too Early Spring, *Stephen Vincent Benèt*
My Sister's Marriage, *Cynthia Rich*
On Saturday Afternoon, *Alan Sillitoe*
A & P, *John Updike*

Detached Autobiography
First Confession, *Frank O'Connor*

Points of Departure: An Anthology of Nonfiction

Edited by James Moffett
(Penguin USA, 1985)

Contents

Factual Articles
TRAVELOGUE
Malta   *Elizabeth Pepper and John Wilcock*
STATE-OF-KNOWLEDGE REPORT
I Sing the Body Electric   *Kathleen McAuliffe*
CHARACTERIZING DESCRIPTION
Water Ouzel   *John Muir*
ENCYCLOPEDIC ENTRY
Mullein   *Michael Moore*
Myth   *Mircea Eliade*

COGITATION

Reflection
Column
Chair Chat   *Jon Carroll*
A Gift to Remember   *Ellen Goodman*
America Needs Poor Soldiers   *Arthur Hoppe*
Revenge is Sour   *George Orwell*
Personal Essay
The Hidden Teacher   *Loren Eiseley*
Seeing   *Annie Dillard*
Book Review
An Anatomy of Melancholy   *Conrad Aiken*
Editorial
The Burning of the Dead   *Lafcadio Hearn*
Ironic Proposal
A Modest Proposal   *Jonathan Swift*
Speech
If We Had Left at Daybreak We Would Be There by
   Now   *Carlos Fuentes*
Thesis and Theory
Thesis
Whiteness   *Herman Melville*
The Functions of War   *edited by Leonard C. Lewin*
Theory
The Dread of Woman   *Karen Horney*
Hypothesis
The Serpent Power   *John Michell*

Active Voices I, II, III, IV

(Boynton/Cook, 1986–1987)

These anthologies of student writing are broken down into categories almost the same as in *Points of Departure*. They don't include the section on nonfictional letters ("Interaction") but add the fictional section "Imagination." In their narrative range, all follow the spectrum of *Points of View*.

These categories differ from those in this book only as alternative ways of breaking down the writing repertory, which I've done one way for teachers and a somewhat different way for students. Also, the samples permit greater elaboration of some types of writing. This room for expansion, plus further thinking on my part, have resulted in some redefinition and refinement of some of the kinds of writing. I trust that working with these consonant but variant frameworks will stimulate readers to think further themselves.

The following tables of contents list the types of writing exemplified, not the titles of the student samples illustrating them (which can be found in the books themselves). Except for captions, actual letters, and some memory-aid or study-aid kind of writing that is just for oneself (which we did not anthologize but which ought to be included), these lists may stand as a fairly full arraying of the writing repertory. None of the assignments are mere exercises, but correspond, rather, to kinds of discourse practiced in our society. I suggest using these lists, which vary only in allowing for some maturity difference, as reference for you and students as you all go about putting together a writing program. The *Teacher's Guide* accompanying *Active Voices* makes some suggestions about this.

Active Voices I (Grades 4–6)

(James Moffett, Marie Carducci Bolchazy, and Barbara Friedberg)

Contents

GROUP	*ASSIGNMENT*
TAKING DOWN (Notation)	GENERAL JOURNAL
	SPECIFIC JOURNAL
	STORY JOURNAL
	JOURNEY JOURNAL
	JOURNAL SUMMARY
LOOKING BACK (Recollection)	MEMORIES
	INCIDENT IN YOUR LIFE

PHASE OF YOUR LIFE
AUTOBIOGRAPHY
EYEWITNESS INCIDENT
MEMOIR OF A PLACE
CANDID CAMERA
SKETCH OF A PERSON

LOOKING INTO   BABY DAYS
                  ORAL STORY
(Investigation)   FAMILY ANECDOTE
                  BIOGRAPHY
                  THE WAY IT USED TO BE
                  FOLK CURES AND RECIPES
                  POLL AND SURVEY
                  INTERVIEW SKETCH
                  ROVING REPORTER
                  FEATURE ARTICLE
                  RESEARCH ARTICLE

THINKING UP   DREAMS
(Imagination)   STORY DRAWN FROM JOURNAL
                  WORD-CHAIN STORY
                  STORY STARTER
                  JOKES
                  RIDDLES
                  YARNS
                  MAKE IT FAMOUS
                  BEING SOMETHING ELSE
                  FILL-IN COMICS
                  PHOTO STORY
                  TALL TALE
                  A SPACE PLACE
                  MAKING UP FROM THE REAL
                  STORY FOR YOUNGER CHILDREN
                  ILLUSTRATED STORYBOOK
                  TWICE-TOLD TALE
                  MIX MEDIA
                  FICTIONAL JOURNAL
                  FICTIONAL CORRESPONDENCE
                  LIMERICK
                  SONG
                  STORY POEM
                  DUOLOG
                  DUOLOG BETWEEN BOOK CHARACTERS

PLAY SCRIPT
RADIO SCRIPT
DO-IT-YOURSELF FOLK TALE
MYTH
FABLE
POEM OF THOUGHT AND FEELING

THINKING OVER　　DIRECTIONS TO MAKE OR DO
(Reflection)　　　　SOMETHING
　　　　　　　　　MINI-ENCYCLOPEDIA
　　　　　　　　　ADVICE LETTER
　　　　　　　　　REVIEW
　　　　　　　　　WISH
　　　　　　　　　EDITORIAL
　　　　　　　　　ESSAY

Active Voices II (Grades 7–9)

(James Moffett and Phyllis Tashlik)

Contents

GROUP	*ASSIGNMENT*
TAKING DOWN (Notation) *Journal and Diary*	WRITER'S JOURNAL REWRITTEN JOURNAL MATERIAL DIARY DIARY SUMMARY
LOOKING BACK (Recollection)	MEMORIES SENSORY MEMORY
Autobiography and Memoir	AUTOBIOGRAPHY: INCIDENT AUTOBIOGRAPHY: PHASE MEMOIR OF ANOTHER PERSON MEMOIR OF A GROUP OR PLACE MEMOIR OF AN EYEWITNESS INCIDENT MEMOIR OF NATURE MEMOIR PROFILE
LOOKING INTO (Investigation)	WRITING UP SENSORY NOTES
Reportage	VISIT INTERVIEW WITH A RELATIVE OR FRIEND

INTERVIEW SKETCH
FAMILY ANECDOTE
HOW IT USED TO BE
FOLK WAYS

Biography   BIOGRAPHY: PHASE
and   ORAL HISTORY PLUS BOOK RESEARCH
Chronicle   CHRONICLE: RECENT
CHRONICLE: HISTORICAL

SURVEY
Other Research   PROFILE OF AN ENTERPRISE
RESEARCH ARTICLE

THINKING UP   DREAMS
(Imagination)   JOKES
RIDDLES
BEING SOMETHING ELSE
CONCRETE AND ACROSTIC POEMS
STORY STARTER
PHOTO STORY
FICTIONAL CORRESPONDENCE
FICTIONAL JOURNAL
FIRST-PERSON FICTION
THIRD-PERSON FICTION
HORROR STORY
Stories   MURDER MYSTERY
SPOOF
FANTASY
SCIENCE FICTION
MYTH
PARABLE
FABLE

DUOLOG
DIALOG FOR THREE OR MORE
EXTERIOR MONOLOG
Plays   INTERIOR MONOLOG
ONE-ACT PLAY
MUSICAL PLAY
SENSORY POEM
PICTURE POEM
MEMORY POEM
Poems   STORY POEM

SONG
POEM OF FEELING AND REFLECTION

THINKING OVER   DIALOG OF IDEAS
(Reflection)   STREAM OF CONSCIOUSNESS
                       STATEMENT THROUGH STORY

                       ADVICE LETTER
Newspaper   DIRECTIONS TO DO OR MAKE
Departments   SOMETHING
                       REVIEW
                       EDITORIAL
                       COLUMN

Essay   TOPIC ESSAY
                       BROAD PERSONAL ESSAY

Active Voices III (Grades 10–12)

(James Moffett, Patricia Wixon, Vincent Wixon, Sheridan Blair, and John Phreaner)

Contents

GROUP	*ASSIGNMENT*
NOTATION	WRITER'S JOURNAL
(Taking Down)	REWRITTEN JOURNAL ENTRY
Journal	DIARY
and	DIARY SUMMARY
Diary	
RECOLLECTION	MEMORIES
(Looking Back)	AUTOBIOGRAPHY: INCIDENT
	AUTOBIOGRAPHY: PHASE
Autobiography	FULL AUTOBIOGRAPHY
and	MEMOIR OF ANOTHER PERSON
Memoir	MEMOIR OF A GROUP OR PLACE
	MEMOIR OF AN EYEWITNESS INCIDENT
	MEMOIR OF NATURE
	MEMOIR PROFILE
INVESTIGATION	WRITING UP SENSORY NOTES
(Looking Into)	
Reportage	PARTICIPANT REPORTAGE
	VISIT
	ORAL STORIES

FAMILY ANECDOTES
INTERVIEW
VISIT PLUS INTERVIEW

Biography
and
Chronicle

BIOGRAPHY: PHASE
BIOGRAPHY: LIFE
CHRONICLE

Case
and
Profile

CASE STUDY
PROFILE: PERSON
PROFILE: ENTERPRISE

Factual
Article

TRADITIONAL LORE
DIRECTIONS TO DO OR MAKE
  SOMETHING

Research
Article

SURVEY
LOCAL RESEARCH
FEATURE ARTICLE
STATE-OF-KNOWLEDGE ARTICLE

IMAGINATION
(Thinking Up)

DREAMS

Plays

DUOLOG
DIALOG FOR THREE OR MORE
EXTERIOR MONOLOG
INTERIOR MONOLOG
ONE-ACT PLAY
FULL-LENGTH PLAY

Stories

STORIES FROM THE NEWS
FICTIONAL ADDITIONS
FICTIONAL CORRESPONDENCE
FICTIONAL JOURNAL
FICTIONAL AUTOBIOGRAPHY
FICTIONAL MEMOIR
THIRD-PERSON FICTION-SINGLE-
  CHARACTER VIEWPOINT
THIRD-PERSON FICTION DUAL-OR
  MULTI-CHARACTER VIEWPOINT
THIRD-PERSON FICTION NO-CHARACTER
  VIEWPOINT
SCIENCE FICTION
MYTH
PARABLE
FABLE

Poems	MEMORY POEMS
	SENSORY POEMS
	PICTURE POEMS
	BORROW-A-LINE POEMS
	POEMS ON PICTURES
	POEMS OF ADDRESS
	BE-A-THING POEMS
	STORY POEMS
	REFLECTIVE POEMS
COGITATION (Thinking Over and Thinking Through)	DIALOG OF IDEAS
	DIALOG CONVERTED TO ESSAY
	STREAM OF CONSCIOUSNESS
	ADVICE LETTER
	STATEMENT THROUGH STORY
	THEMATIC COLLECTION OF INCIDENTS
	PERSONAL ESSAY
	GENERALIZATION SUPPORTED BY INSTANCES
	EDITORIAL
	REVIEW
	DESCRIPTION/DEFINITION
	COMPARISON
	EVALUATION
	CAUSAL ANALYSIS
	TEXTUAL INTERPRETATION

Active Voices IV (College)

(James Moffett, Miriam Baker, and Charles Cooper)

Contents

GROUP	ASSIGNMENT
NOTATION (Taking Down) *Journal and Diary*	WRITER'S JOURNAL
	REWRITTEN JOURNAL ENTRY
	DIARY
	DIARY SUMMARY
RECOLLECTION (Looking Back)	MEMORIES
	AUTOBIOGRAPHY: INCIDENT
	AUTOBIOGRAPHY: PHASE

Autobiography *and* *Memoir*	MEMOIR OF ANOTHER PERSON MEMOIR OF A GROUP OR PLACE MEMOIR OF AN EYEWITNESS INCIDENT MEMOIR OF NATURE MEMOIR PROFILE
INVESTIGATION (Looking Into) *Reportage*	VISIT INTERVIEW ORAL HISTORY FAMILY HISTORY VISIT PLUS INTERVIEW
Biography *and* *Chronicle*	BIOGRAPHY: INCIDENT BIOGRAPHY: PHASE BIOGRAPHY: LIFE CHRONICLE
Case and *Profile*	CASE: INDIVIDUAL CASE: GROUP PROFILE
Factual Research *Articles*	DIRECTIONS FOR HOW TO DO OR MAKE SOMETHING STATE-OF-KNOWLEDGE ARTICLE SURVEY AND RESEARCH RESEARCH GENERALIZATION
IMAGINATION (Thinking Up) *Plays*	DREAMS DUOLOG TRIOLOG EXTERIOR MONOLOG INTERIOR MONOLOG ONE-ACT PLAY MIXING TECHNIQUES FICTIONAL CORRESPONDENCE FICTIONAL DIARY SUBJECTIVE FICTIONAL AUTOBIOGRAPHY DETACHED FICTIONAL AUTOBIOGRAPHY

Fiction	THIRD-PERSON, SINGLE-CHARACTER
	  VIEWPOINT
	THIRD-PERSON, DUAL-CHARACTER
	  VIEWPOINT

THIRD-PERSON, MULTIPLE-CHARACTER
VIEWPOINT

Folk Tales	TALL TALES LEGEND MYTH PARABLE FABLE
Poetry	SENSORY POEMS MEMORY POEMS SONGS BE-A-THING POEMS FUNCTION POEMS POEMS OF ADDRESS REFLECTIVE POEMS
COGITATION (Thinking Over and Thinking Through) *Informal* *Essay*	DIALOG OF IDEAS DIALOG CONVERTED TO ESSAY STREAM OF CONSCIOUSNESS MEDITATIVE REFLECTION STATEMENT THROUGH STORY THEMATIC COLLECTION OF INCIDENTS GENERALIZATION ABOUT ONESELF GENERALIZATION ABOUT ANYTHING PERSONAL ESSAY COLUMN EDITORIAL REVIEW
Formal *Essay*	DESCRIPTION/DEFINITION COMPARISON EVALUATION TEXTUAL INTERPRETATION CAUSAL ANALYSIS

COLLATERAL READING
FOR TEACHERS

A fuller treatment of the theory from which this program springs can be found in *Teaching the Universe of Discourse* (Boynton/Cook, 1983), which in addition to delineating an abstractive hierarchy embracing the total curriculum includes chapters on composition and grammar in particular.

Classroom procedures for teaching writing are detailed in many chapters in *Student-Centered Language Arts, K-12*, co-authored with Betty Jane Wagner (fourth edition, Boynton/Cook, 1992). It mixes writing with other activities. I would feel more comfortable if teachers were at least familiar with this integrated language arts curriculum, because writing should not be taught in isolation from the many other language activities, described there, that provide writing with warm-ups and follow-ups. That book contains chapters on discussing, improvising, performing texts, and becoming literate. Besides some reporting on the results of the original writing experiments, it includes some other writing assignments that do not fit handily into the frame of reference of this program, which was never intended to be a complete writing curriculum but rather a selective series allowing youngsters to flourish through writing about their experience while at the same time preparing them to write critically about ideas and information presented to them by others. Imaginative writing is elaborated much more there than here.

Finally, *Coming on Center: Essays in English Education* (Boynton/Cook, second edition, 1988) provides further elaboration and perspective on writing and allied language activities.

Bridges
FROM PERSONAL WRITING
TO THE FORMAL ESSAY*

They say that writing was invented about five thousand years ago. That may be so, but it was only discovered about ten years ago in American schools, thanks to the National Writing Project movement. I don't usually feel obliged as a speaker to start with a joke. I've found from experience that I usually commit enough goofs, glitches, and faux pas that it is unnecessary to schedule comic relief. But I did come by a joke, very recently, that I can rationalize. I heard a speaker who was a humorous storyteller, a kind of cracker barrel raconteur. In one of his jokes, he told of a family from the backwoods of Virginia. There was a boy who had grown up to be about ten or eleven and had never said a word. Everyone grew accustomed to this, but one night as they were sitting around the dinner table, the boy suddenly said, "There's too many lumps in the gravy."

They looked over at him absolutely flabbergasted and said, "If you could talk, how come you haven't said anything before?"

He replied, "Everything has been pretty good up till now."

I submit that there's a whole theory of language function secreted within this joke if you bother to extract it.

A speaker has a choice of whether to say something general and inspirational and uplifting, or to say something of some practical value. For better or for worse, I have opted for the latter. My subject is how writing teachers get students from the personal-experience theme, with its many colloquial terms, to the formal essay. This seems to be a national issue. We are under pressure to do the thing that colleges seem to value most—to teach the kind of essay that corresponds to term papers or essay questions. Colleges emphasize this because it is part of their testing program, and this pressure passes all the way down to the elementary school. I believe we are gearing up for this sort

* The text that appears here is a modified version of a transcript of a talk from notes that I gave as part of the Center for the Study of Writing Seminar Series, published by the Center as Occasional Paper No. 9, March, 1989.

of thing far too early. At any rate, this tends to determine the bent of the writing curriculum we have. What I'm going to try to aim at here are ways of doing justice to other kinds of writing that will at the same time prepare for what colleges want.

There are two main ways I think we can bridge from the personal narrative to kinds of informal and formal essays. One is by way of intervening kinds of discourse, kinds of writing, that students might practice in between personal writing and essay writing, kinds of discourse that schools could take much more advantage of. The other way is by parlaying personal writing directly into essay. I'll try to give some examples of that later. I like the term "parlay." It comes from the French "to speak," but in Anglicized use it means to transform something on into something else and that's exactly what we are trying to do here in getting from personal writing to essay writing. We will look for ways of parlaying first-person narrative into essays.

I've been involved a good while in anthologizing student writing. This work has come out in four books called *Active Voices I, II, III*, and *IV*. These are anthologies of student writing. All they have in them are brief directions and samples of student writings to illustrate the assignments. The reason the project lasted longer than I would have liked is that I had difficulty getting writing in certain categories. That's one of the things I hope to emphasize—we don't ask for a broad variety of writing from our students.

I didn't go for just the top students or top schools, and I didn't run national contests. I worked partly through National Writing Project sites here and there, and partly from other contacts I had from previous curriculum work. I asked some teachers to send student writing to me from a variety of levels and backgrounds. Some of the pieces were very accomplished, and some authors, as you will see, are not so very experienced. All the selections have vitality, and they illustrate the kind of writing that I thought other students would appreciate and want to emulate.

The idea is that you use former students' writing to work with current students. Many teachers are doing this on their own, and I think that's excellent. I would certainly encourage that. You can array for students what the various kinds of writing look like when done by their peers. I also anthologize professional writing, but the problem with professional writing is that it is so intimidating that students sometimes do not identify with those writers. But I believe in using both.

In putting together these anthologies of students' writing I worked across the board, up and down all the grades, from elementary school into college. I wanted a repertory that would hold good for all the years. I didn't invent tricky assignments or cute stuff to write; I simply looked at what's going on outside of school. If school is a preparation for life, let's see what's going on out there. What do people outside of school who practice writing really do? These samples represent the main repertory of writing possibilities, more certainly than can be done in a single year. Although I won't go into how to use the repertory (a whole subject in itself), I do want to suggest that it can be used to individualize writing, which I think we should do much more.

Figure 1 is my way of breaking down the main kinds of writing, the writing repertory, into five groupings. At the bottom is a category called *Noting Down*. The reason it's at the bottom is that journals, logs, diaries, and all sorts of notes are really the base for the kinds of writings above. I think you understand what I mean by the base. You write down things, and later you can write them up. This is a way of garnering material, jotting things down. Journalists write down everything that might possibly be used later as ideas for writing. At first, they plan to use most of it, but they usually just use some of it. Many professionals take field notes and lab notes. They accumulate materials that they write up into one of the above forms on the schema.

At the next level I have two groupings or very important domains of discourse called *Looking Back* and *Looking Into*. The one on the left is undoubtedly a lot more familiar to teachers, for that's really where you have the personal-experience themes, the first-person narrative. I use the traditional terms "autobiography," which is focused on the author, and "memoir," which is focused on others. So those two represent a shift of focus, and we are already on our way to essay. Memoir is somewhere between personal writing and essay, precisely because of that shift of focus from author to other. The less familiar category, *Looking Into* (Investigation)—which deserves a lot of attention it isn't getting—is reportage and research. It includes traditional third-person types like "biography" and "chronicle" as well as journalistic forms like "cases," "profiles," "factual articles" and "feature articles." Investigation is an important domain in our society, for I believe most people who read are getting their information and ideas through newspapers and magazines and certain kinds of nonfiction books. In fact, many literary writers and novelists, such as Joan Didion and Norman Mailer, sometimes shift back and forth from fiction to nonfiction. Investigation deserves a lot of attention, in part because it has the attention of some of our major writers but also because this writing has gotten very good in our day.

I think people with a literature background are apt to look disdainfully at journalism. We create this little specialty of journalism, and it goes off in a box on the shelf, available only to a few students who elect it. But it ought to be mainstreamed, and I'll try to explain why.

Figure 1. Kinds of Writing

THINKING UP
(Imagination)

Fiction
Plays
Poetry

THINKING OVER/THINKING THROUGH
(Cogitation)

Column
Editorial
Review
Personal essay
Thesis essay

LOOKING BACK
(Recollection)

Autobiography
Memoir

LOOKING INTO
(Investigation)

Biography
Chronicle
Case
Profile
Factual article
Feature article

NOTING DOWN
(Notation)

Journal
Diary
Logs

Reportage and research represent an important bridge between personal writing and transpersonal writing. (I don't like the term "impersonal." It sounds like nobody's home: there's no face, no voice—just some sort of ghost writing—so I use the term "transpersonal.") I had the most difficulty getting writing in this category, and it is fascinating to think about why schools have neglected the main way to bridge between first-person writing and essay writing.

I think you will agree that investigative writing has been almost universally ignored in the schools. There are many reasons, some of them practical, some having to do with our backgrounds. Even very good teachers, who have a strong background in writing, often don't bother with it. What I found is that most teachers, even very good writing teachers, work with only a few kinds of writing. I am sure they will say they don't have time for more, and it may very well be true. We need to understand why even the best teachers don't require a broader range of writing from their students.

There's a lot to be said about *Looking Into* precisely because we haven't been trained to deal with it, unless you happen to have had some journalism experience. Most teachers probably haven't written in this area, so they don't feel too comfortable with it. Nevertheless, we all have done this kind of reading, *New Yorker* reportage and the excellent kind of reportage that we often get in newspapers and magazines. We feel confident to assess this, so I think we shouldn't feel so wary about assigning student writing in that area.

What do you do when you do investigative writing? You go look, you go ask, or you go look it up—three main things that reporters and researchers do. They go on site, visit, observe, and take notes. Or they interview one or many people, and again they take notes. Or what they can't get from looking and asking they go look up and see what other people have said about this. They go to records, documents, books and so on. This is where the library research comes in. As you notice, what happens here is that you move more and more from first-hand into second-hand information, and that's part of the movement from personal writing to essay writing.

From first person you can draw an arrow, if you wish, going from the left over to the right in Figure 1, from *Looking Back to Looking Into*. One of the movements involved is in that direction, going from first person to third person, from writing about self to writing about others, and from first-hand information to second- and third-hand information. I believe this is a very natural movement.

Let's go to the top level. The reason it's above is that *Looking Back* and *Looking Into* form a concrete data base for these other two. The memory is a tremendous storehouse of materials that all professional writers use. It's not narcissistic or solipsistic or just about oneself; it's about all sorts of things. If you think of your own memories, you will recognize that they are about everything, everything you ever had a chance to observe, experience, or participate in. The memory has all sorts of potentialities for the transpersonal writing that goes into essay. The other domain, *Looking Into* (Investigation), includes many sources of materials outside oneself. These are the two main sources on which the top two categories are built.

Thinking Up (Imagination) is most familiar to English teachers, who generally have a literature background. It's what we call "creative writing," but I don't like that term and I never use it. In fact, I never use the word "creative." It sounds sentimental. Creative writing is one of those specialities I wish we didn't have. I wish we would mainstream the writing of fiction into the composition program and not regard it as a specialty like journalism. Few kids will ever take such a specialty, and as a result we remove again one of the main bridges into essay writing.

We generally think of all fiction writing—poetry, plays, short stories—as being very different from the writing of ideas. I regard *all* writing as idea writing. To me the difference is not whether the writing has ideas but how buried the ideas are, how implicit or explicit the ideas are. In literature and recollection, the ideas are more implicit. They are there, but they are embodied, incarnated in personages, incidents, and events. If this is not true of literature, why do we have students digging for meaning all the time? Why do we have them chasing symbols and doing vivisections of poems and postmortems on novels, digging, digging, digging, all the time for meaning?

Here is a great irony. We have a curriculum in which students *write exposition*; but when they read, they *read literature*. We should have them do *both* types of reading and writing. It's very important for them to have the chance to do some writing in these figurative, fictional modes, because for one thing, these modes are an implicit way of stating ideas. All stories are statements. We can use the term "conclusion" for both fiction and nonfiction. In stories, the conclusions are inherent in the "logic of the events." If that's not true, then we should quit having kids analyzing novels and plays for their meaning.

It is evident that folk literature—fables, parables, legends, and myths—exist mainly to convey ideas, but they convey them in a kind of subconscious or preconscious way. Today we have a heavy industry in analyzing myths. We have whole disciplines mining myths for their meaning—Jungian analysts and anthropologists and literary critics. Legends, fables, parables, and myths all exist as stories that make statements. The fable is right on the hinge between story and statement because the meaning is distilled out as moral at the end. It is interesting to look at folk literature because it tells you a little more clearly about what's going on in modern literature that we are more familiar with.

Let's move into a consideration of the category labeled *Thinking Over/ Thinking Through*. I am all for the essay, and I think we should do as much of it as we can. However, I believe that if we move into it developmentally we will get better results. This category includes "Column," "Editorial," and "Review," the journalistic forms of essay. I imagine most people read essays of this sort, and those who are writing them are writing in these journalistic forms. Many of them do exactly what we want students to do in writing—make a generalization and then support it with examples, documentation, and illustrations.

There are many avenues to this, two of which are *Investigation* and *Imagination*. A third way is to go directly from *Recollection* up into *Cogitation*, because memory is a main source of ideas. All we have to do is extrapolate memories, which is what many essayists do. It always amuses me that George Orwell's "Shooting an Elephant" has been anthologized *ad nauseam* in all the college anthologies under Essay. If a student had written it, it would be called a personal-experience theme. Most of it is narrative, first-person, telling about how he was compelled to shoot an elephant against his will under pressure of the group when he was in civil service in Burma. He knew how to extract and extrapolate the transpersonal aspect of his personal experience so that in the end we think of it as an essay, although it is a piece of autobiography. But the point is that it is very hard to tell the difference because *memory is one of the main routes to get into the essay.*

What I am suggesting here is that all writing is thinking; it is simply a question of whether the thinking is explicit or implicit. What I suggest is that on the left side of Figure 1, the thinking is implicit and on the right side, it is explicit. Exposition, argumentation, persuasion are on the right-hand side. What we call persuasion and argumentation are not precise terms but general terms for kinds of thesis essay writing. All of the group called *Looking Into* is expository. It bridges into argumentation and persuasion because that is the natural effect of reportage, research, and journalism. After a while an investigator tends not only to gather information but to generalize it, to argue points. The reporter on the beat becomes a columnist in print media, a "commentator" in broadcast journalism. So draw another arrow from Investigation to Cogitation.

The implicit (categories on the left side) roughly corresponds to the functioning of the right hemisphere of the brain, and the explicit (categories on the right side) to the functioning of the left hemisphere. But the trouble with that is that it gets to be a little too neat. First thing you know, we'll be back to that awful division of Bloom's into affective and cognitive, which I think is one of the abominations of educational movements. It's not the case that one hemisphere of the brain is cognitive and the other affective, of having mushy emotion on one hand and dry rationality on the other. Both hemispheres—and both the implicit and explicit—are ways of cognizing. They are both cognitive. It is not that half the head is emotional and the other half rational. It is a disservice to education that we ever accepted that kind of dichotomy.

The only other general thing I would say about the schema in Figure 1 is that the movement, if you go upward here, is generally inductive. That is, it works from particulars to generalities, moving from the concrete particulars of personal experience and narrative ("*once* upon a time") to generality, which is not "once upon a time" but *any* time. We speak of the "present tense of generalization" in grammar, and that is exactly what essay is. So this movement from the concrete particulars to the generalities is an inductive movement in terms of logic. I believe that we have not offered in writing programs enough opportunities to students to work inductively, but that is the way they build their own knowledge structures.

There is a lot of hue and cry today about "thinking"; the buzz word is "critical thinking." If we look seriously at thinking and writing, we soon come to realize that we don't have to add thinking because it is already part and parcel of writing. If we are serious about thinking, we will allow students to work far more inductively than they have in the past, building up from sources of plenty instead of employing a strategy of working from scarcity. I will explain what I mean by that. The deductive approach is to work from the top down, from the higher level abstractions to the lower. If you are given a topic, or if you choose a topic, or if the essay exam gives you some quotation and you are supposed to refute or support it, and your grade is on the line, then you start at a higher generalization and go downward, looking for something to support or illustrate the generalization. That is what I call a wrong strategy, working from scarcity. What we should work from is plenty, from too much material, so much that you have to waste it, throw some of it away, edit it, winnow it out—in short, compose and select, abstract. Memories and investigations represent materials both inside and outside, wealthy positions, a source of plenty and not a position of scarcity. That sort of wrong-headed strategy comes from working too deductively, starting students at high-level abstract topics, or generalities, and then asking them to go down. It puts us in the position of being professional naggers. We are nagging for details, nagging for evidence, nagging for support, illustrations, and examples, no matter what the kind of writing. This shouldn't happen. It is one of those problems to which we think up brilliant solutions, but it is a stupid problem. It comes from wanting to control the subject matter of student writing and from riding herd on essay before honoring other kinds of writing. If we really want to teach thinking and writing together and get from personal experience to essay, then we should emphasize inductive thinking, which is itself a bridge to deductive thinking.

Now I would like to turn to some selections from student writing. What I want to emphasize here is the parlaying from personal-experience writing directly into the essay, which I think is a very natural movement if we know how to work it. I try to get my students (who are all teachers, by the way, with a lot of experience) to think about what is generic in some of their personal experience. I ask them to choose a personal incident in their life, something interesting, and then to write about it. Then I ask, "Of what is this incident a metaphor?" Maybe nothing will come, but when it does, you are on the road to an essay.

Of what is this personal incident a metaphor? Or an emblem or symbol? What does it represent? Of what type is it a token? As soon as you begin writing about types, through the tokens, through the particulars, you are dealing with what essay essentially consists of, which is coordinating an idea with an incident or instance.

Another way is to pluralize personal experiences. I sometimes ask, "Can you think of other incidents, other experiences, to go with this one? Here you would put together a collection, a category of incidents or experiences, which all show the same thing, which all point the same way. They go together, and in that you have your thesis idea. That is the inductive approach. You transpersonalize by including incidents and experiences not just from your personal memories but from what you've heard from other people and what you've read, thus connecting incidents in your own life with incidents in the lives of characters in fiction and drama and of other people you know about. Pluralizing is generalizing.

Now the samples. The first couple are from senior high, grades 10 to 12. The first is an Autobiographical Incident, something very specific that happened in a very small time and space, something that happened one day.

WONDER WOMAN STRIKES AGAIN
VICKI BILIK

It was Monday, the first day of kindergarten after Easter vacation. School had gone well that day. I arrived early that morning with a little baggie full of left-over jellybeans in my lunch. A complete repertoire of stories for my friends, ranging from what the Easter Bunny brought me to the egg hunt in my grandmother's backyard.

The day had gone well. I had convinced all my classmates that I had received the biggest Easter basket of all of them, and I even succeeded in trading a mere two jellybeans for an entire marshmallow bunny. I was shrewd and unfeeling in my business affairs. So, there I was in front of the school, waiting for my mother and contemplating the day's victories. All of a sudden, a sparkle caught my eye. I looked down and there they were, my brand new, black, patent leather shoes, the pride of Miss Bradey's kindergarten class. I had got them to wear on Easter Sunday along with my brand new dress. I was so proud of them.

As I sat there admiring my prized possessions, I felt a shadow fall upon me. I looked up, and there was Jeffrey Wilson. He thought he was so cool just because he was in first grade and I was only in kindergarten. For absolutely no reason at all he looked down and sneered.

"Those are the ugliest shoes I've ever seen!" Then if that insult to my precious shoes wasn't enough, he leaned over and *spit* on them.

I felt the tears rush to my eyes, but I held them back. I wasn't going to let that beast know how deeply he had hurt me.

Suddenly I became aware of something heavy in my right hand. Of course! My Wonder Woman lunch box! Wonder Woman wouldn't let me down. I reached my right arm back and then swung forward, Wonder Woman hitting Jeffrey in the face with all her might.

"That'll show that creep!" I thought.

Just as I watched Jeffrey go crying into the boys' bathroom, my mother pulled up in the station wagon. I got in the car and relaxed against the seat. Defending one's honor is very hard work, you know.[1]

Of course, you can see this is a very aware girl. She knows exactly what she is doing. The story includes a very brave picture of a not so admirable side of herself, at least back when she was in kindergarten. You can see she doesn't make many explicit statements; this is pure story. And yet it is full of so many ideas, so many potentialities, so many generalizations you could make if you wanted to. You could add other incidents that would lead to more general notions about boys and girls of that age, or their relationships, or relationships between the sexes generally, or about smugness and complacency, or about unwittingly tempting other people. You see so many potential themes.

It's always interesting to me that we use the term "theme" for any type of student writing. "Theme" means a kind of thesis or a generalization. I think essay consists mainly of bringing out some of these latent ideas.

The next piece is from a high school boy who lives in rural Oregon, east of the Cascade Mountains. It is a Memoir of Nature, as I call the assignment.

[1] *Active Voices III*, p. 36.

COUGARS AT BAY
SCOTT STEPHENS

About three years ago I witnessed something very few city folks get to see.

I was archery hunting in a remote canyon, known to most people as Fiddlers Hell. This was not irregular at all since Doug Anderson and I hunted there quite often. It's a steep canyon that most people won't dare to venture into.

I didn't quite know what I was doing there. I saw many deer and elk and didn't even bother to shoot.

About noon I stopped to rest on a large rock. I was sitting there enjoying the scenery, when I spotted a slight movement in the brush. I was hoping to see a big bull elk.

To my surprise two full grown cougars strolled out into the meadow. They were playing happily, wrestling with each other.

The wind was blowing in my face and I was sitting above them. As long as I was still I could watch them play.

They played in the meadow for about an hour, and then as if a signal from nature beckoned to them, they raced off. I wasn't quite sure what made them run off. I attempted to follow them.

As I stepped off my rock, I caught a faint sound of braying dogs. Then I knew. Poachers! I thought for sure the cats would be shot.

I ran up on the ridge, leaving my bow lying on the ground. I spotted the dogs. I was shocked. These were no pure-bred hunting dogs used by poachers. Instead, they were a mangy crew of about seven dogs, led by a big redbone. It was the wild pack that I had heard so much about. I spotted the cougars just ahead of the pack. One cougar climbed a tree, the other prepared to fight. With a rock cliff at its back and the pack at its front, it fought.

I ran back to get my bow. When I reached the fight one cougar and five dogs lay dead. The other two dogs ran off. I went up to the cougar. It was a large male. The female was still in the tree.

I never understood why the male didn't tree, or why the female didn't help.

About three months later I figured it out. In the first place if he had climbed the tree the dogs would have waited for them to starve. And the male fought the dogs to give the female a chance for her life; she was bearing young. I've often gone back

to Fiddlers Hell to look for the cougars, but I've never found them. [2]

One of the things interesting to me about this piece is that the writer is always trying to figure out things. He is thinking about what he observes. The story is straightforwardly told by a boy who tuned into nature and was a good observer. He probably hunts just as an excuse to get out there in nature and observe it. He really didn't do any hunting here, but he's thinking about what he observes. I believe this is the main thing that makes an essay successful.

As you can see, this writing is not really focused on the author himself. It's told in the first person, but it's focused on what he's looking at. So it is on its way to exposition because it tells you about what goes on in the world; it's information and reflection.

The next piece is from an eighth-grader. It is a poll from that domain call *Investigation*. Essentially you think of some question you want answered and then go out and find the answer. Kids think of something they want to know more about, and the teacher helps them find out how to know more about it. The author wanted to know more about what people think about nuclear energy. This piece is from Spanish Harlem, New York City, where we've collected a lot of writing from junior high.

A POLL ON NUCLEAR ENERGY
GEMMA DIGRAZIA

This poll was conducted mainly among middle-class New Yorkers. Almost all of the adults had a college education. The majority of them live on the Upper West Side. There was an equal amount of females and males. Most people who answered were over forty or under twenty.

The questions asked were:

1. **Do you think nuclear energy is necessary as an alternative energy source? If no: What are the alternatives?**
   36% thought nuclear energy was necessary. All of them mentioned that other energy sources would run out.

[2] *Active Voices III*, pp. 75–76.

64% said it wasn't necessary. Energy alternatives they listed were: coal, solar, waterpower, and conservation of existing energy.

2. **Describe what you think the effects of radioactivity on humans are.** All people mentioned some physical symptoms as effects of radiation and radioactivity. These are:

symptoms	% of people who mentioned each symptom
death	60%
genetic damage	58%
radiation sickness	56%
general sickness	52%
cancer	36%
sterility	12%

3. **Do you think the public is fully informed about nuclear hazards and safety?**

   All said no, the public wasn't fully informed.

   25% said no because they think most people aren't educated enough to understand the problems of nuclear energy.

   50% said no, because they think information is deliberately withheld in lies and coverups by the government and nuclear energy people.

   5% said they think nuclear energy is too technical and complex for almost everybody to understand.

   20% said the public is not told everything because there is no reason to panic them when they can't do anything about it.

4. **Would you know what to do in case of a nuclear disaster (i.e., melt-down) in your area?**

   55% said no.

   45% said yes. Those who don't feel nuclear energy is dangerous had faith in the authorities to tell them how to avoid harm. Everyone else was afraid of dying and said they would run or hide, listen to T.V./radio but not believe everything they heard, or hold their loved ones and pets.

5. **Do you think that children should be educated to the benefits and dangers of nuclear energy? Why or why not?**

2% said no, people at that age shouldn't be burdened with such things.

98% said yes, they are our future. Future decisions depend on them.

Yes, so they are more fully informed about the world we live in.

Some people wrote yes, though wait until they're old enough.

6. Do you think you can do anything to educate others about nuclear energy?

   18% said no, they were not educated enough themselves to teach about it.

   12% said yes, educate people to its benefits.

   60% said yes, they would tell people the facts and were sure that these would convince them of their dangers.

7. Are you in favor of using nuclear energy?

   12% said yes only if for medical purposes or if safety is drastically improved.

   48% said yes, either now or in the future. Most of these people thought it was necessary to have nuclear energy and it was just a matter of making it safer.

   40% said no, because of obvious dangers and lack of possible safety ever.

8. Do you think we can have safe nuclear energy?

   42% said no because of either total unsafeness of any nuclear energy or because those in control will push it on us before it can be made safe.

   30% said maybe. They said this because of lack of information or belief that it *can* be safe, but it might be safe long after it is in use.

   28% said yes. These people believe either that nuclear energy is safe now or will be very soon.

The people who were for nuclear energy contradicted themselves a bit on the question that asked if you think the public is fully informed on nuclear energy. All of them thought that not all the information about nuclear energy was available to the public, yet they all thought that they had enough information to feel safe and in favor.

The people who were unsure felt they didn't know enough.

The people against nuclear energy also felt that information was kept from them. One of the issues everyone agreed upon was the issue of the public's awareness of the information about nuclear energy. They all seem to think we need to know more.

Everyone thought that a nuclear energy accident would be harmful to people, and yet some people felt nuclear energy was safe or will be soon. And these people were in favor of using nuclear energy as an energy source.

Before I took the poll I had some ideas of what kinds of answers would be given back to me. I had hoped that most of the people would have been against nuclear energy, but the majority of the people were for nuclear energy. Another thing that surprised me was the amount of people who were uniformed or unsure. I had hoped that people would be surer on an issue like this.

From this poll I have learned a lot. I have learned how people have such different opinions from each other and how rigid some people are. The most surprising thing is that people have such opposite opinions while using the same information to get their opinions.[3]

That's not a bad conclusion. The writer arrived at it inductively from her own information. She did the leg work to find out what people thought about something. She thought about what they said; she related responses to the questions and drew her own conclusions.

Next is a piece from elementary school. I use these domains for all grades, but it is obvious that in the lower grades you are not going to get as much of some kinds of writing. For example, you wouldn't expect a lot of thesis writing in the elementary school. I think it should be available for those who can, and in this way individualization can occur. Kids can do extraordinary things in elementary school, but you shouldn't insist that they all do the same thing at the same time. Those who can should go ahead and do it. Some groups will be writing at one level, some at other levels. There are many possibilities for expository and persuasive writing, and the essay included here, a review, goes into only some of those possibilities.

[3] *Active Voices II*, pp. 110–112.

CAT CALLS
NINA BILLONE

Suddenly the whole stage turned red, and colored lights flashed on and off. Two cats cautiously crawled out of a pipe. The trunk to a broken-down car opened with a creak, while more cats filled the stage.

My mother and I had seats in the mezzanine, which is just above the first floor of the Schubert Theater in Chicago. I was extremely excited because I was watching *Cats*.

The stage was decorated like a junkyard. There were four Rice Krispies cereal boxes about two feet high, a tennis racket, and a garbage can, but best of all there was a tire that was about four feet around.

After minutes of dancing, the cats all went back to their hiding places except one. He started singing, "I have a Gumby Cat in mind. Her name is Jenny Anny Dots. Her coat is of the tabby kind with tiger stripes and leopard spots. . . ." As he sang, the trunk to the car opened. Inside was a cat with tiger stripes and leopard spots acting out every move that the cat sang about Jenny Anny Dots.

Many songs went by such as "Growl Tiger, Gus" (the theater cat), "Mongojerrie" and "Rumpleteazer," etc.

Then a very interesting song came on, "The Rum Tum Tugger," which started out, "The Rum Tum Tugger is a curious cat. . . ." The Rum Tum Tugger was a teenage cat whose coat was black and stuck to his body. I decided he was my favorite cat. He acted a lot like our cat Benjy. The play ended.

On the way home I saw in the back seat of the car with my mind full of scenes from the wonderful play I had just seen.

I like cats a lot, and seeing *Cats* made me realize that other people understand cats the way I do and know that they are like people.[4]

Of course some of those "other people" include T. S. Eliot. She's in good company. This girl doesn't do everything that can be done in a

---

[4] *Active Voices I*, pp. 257–258.

review but she comes to some generalizations in the end, and elementary kids should have some opportunities for writing real reviews. The form will grow as they grow.

Finally a couple of samples of what we call personal essay, which is not a very specific category, but much of our best literary writing falls into this category, from the eighteenth century on through to modern authors.

The following is from junior high school.

FUNNY FEELINGS
JENNIFER LEVI

Lately, walking down the street has not been the most pleasant thing for me to do. I feel very self-conscious because men are always looking and saying things to me. I don't think I do or say or wear anything to get myself noticed. I think it is disgusting that men feel that they have the right to say things to women they don't even know. I don't think they know how it makes women feel; I don't even think they care. All they care about is themselves and having their fun.

It makes me angry, but at the same time it makes me scared. It makes me angry that they can make me feel like I can not walk around without being watched. It makes me scared because at any given moment they might hurt me.

I remember when I was just starting to develop and I was very embarrassed about it. There was only one other girl in my class that had started to develop too. I remember hearing some boys in my class talking about their bodies—they were *so* proud about their bodies, but I never really talked to any of my friends about it then. Now we sometimes talk about it, but not a lot. It seems like boys always talk about their bodies. Sometimes I even get embarrassed listening to them talking about their own bodies.

I felt real weird because in one way I was being told to be showy about my body from movies and TV. At the same time I was being told to be quiet about my body from my own fear of what other people would think. For a while I was very confused until I finally decided to go with my own feelings. Now I do not show it and I do not hide it. I just wear what I want and I do what I want to do. I don't let my fear or what I see interfere with what I do or wear.

I think that as you grow up you become less ashamed and

more proud of your body (male or female). I know that men, well at least the men on the street, are very proud and showy of their bodies. Some women, the ones on TV and in movies, are showy, and some women just don't do anything either way, like me.

I know that I can not make the men on the street stop looking and saying weird things to me; all I *can* do is not make them or anyone else feel the way they've made me feel.[5]

This could have been put in fictional form or in a poem. In fact I found that a lot of what I really felt were essays were done as poems in junior high. I included some of them under the category of essay because that's what they were, and then it occurred to me that poetry may be a natural way for junior high kids to express some of their emerging generalizations.

I'm going to end with a personal essay written by one of my students at the Bread Loaf School of English in Vermont, herself an experienced teacher. What she does here is to pluralize personal experiences, tell two incidents that show the same thing. She does here exactly what Orwell does in an essay, "Revenge Is Sour,"° which is virtually unknown.

As you know, Orwell was a reporter or journalist. In World War II, he went in to Europe right behind the liberation forces, with other journalists. From that experience he did a piece called "Revenge is Sour," based of course on one of our platitudes, revenge is sweet. So his thesis is his title. He tells two incidents which he witnessed that document his point. The first incident occurred somewhere in France when he was with another journalist. The American troops had rounded up some SS officers who were a miserable-looking lot. There was one in particular who had clubfeet and looked psychotic. A Jewish American officer came up and began kicking the SS officer. The American officer said he felt that this was his moment when revenge would be sweet. But Orwell says that when that moment comes it isn't sweet; you think the victory is going to be sweet when you are helpless and hapless and out of power, when you are the victim. When you're back in power, you get revenge, but it really isn't sweet. That's what Orwell is saying. Then he related that to punishment in Germany after World War II, to events such as the Nuremberg trials. He told of a second incident in which he and a Belgian journalist were entering Stuttgart

[5] *Active Voices II*, p. 310.

just after the forces had gone in. The Belgian journalist was prepared to hate the Germans when he saw them—"the Boches," he called them, using the old World War I term. When he saw a dead German soldier on the way in, he noticed that somebody had strewn a spray of lilacs over the body, perhaps as a kind of funeral gesture. It was the first dead person the other reporter had even seen. By the time he had actually seen German prisoners, he wasn't able to savor their downfall as he thought he would. He gave them coffee instead.

This construction is very similar to what we will read next. The writer was not emulating the Orwell essay at all. Our class hadn't read it; she just came up with it spontaneously. She put together two incidents which she felt showed the same thing.

A WORK OF ART
SHIRLEY RAU

I recently served on a panel on a three-day writing conference in Boise, Idaho. Eight teachers of English from grade school through college were arranged in a small semi-circle on a stage, responding to questions from conference participants. Toward the end of the afternoon, everyone was getting tired. We were all thinking about the half hour that remained between us and release from the cramped auditorium. Valorie leaned toward the small hand-held mike with a three by five card, the last question from her discussion group: "What is a teacher's responsibility when a student turns in writing that is confessional or that reflects a troubled perspective?" Her voice reverberated as I met the blank eyes of those opposite from me. Pat took the mike:

"The best thing to do is treat the piece as a work of art and comment on it as such. We are not trained to deal with counseling matters." Her businesslike finality signaled another panel member to go on to the next question. The rest of the section was a blur. My mind kept turning over and over "treat the piece as a work of art." That clinical, rubber-glove theory of dealing with writing was echoed by members of my own department. Literary majors all, they analyzed narrative perspective, imagery, character, plot, genre and theme. They analyzed everything in literature except its connection to reality.

Last year every student in my class kept a literary response journal. **Charlotte Britton's journal was filled with poetry, which reflected her fragility and sensitivity. Each week writing groups met to share sections of the journals for comments. The poem that Charlotte shared in February was stark, devoid of the romantic softness so typical in her writing. And though I heard the poem that day and have read it many times since, I can only remember torn snatches:**

> **a dove**
> **the clang of a metal door**
> **a gun**
> **the question to one who remains**

I don't remember exactly how the writing group responded; perhaps we didn't, perhaps the words of her poem turned over and over in our minds until the businesslike finality of some response signaled another reader to go on to the next piece. One week after writing the poem, Charlotte went into the bathroom between classes and shot herself in the chest. She lived through the suicide attempt but I've died it a thousand times.[6]

What the author has done here is put together two instances of teachers distancing themselves from student emotion, and she has put them together, exactly as Orwell did, to illustrate a thesis, which she too states in her title, "A Work of Art," though more obliquely than Orwell.

My own assignment today was to talk about how students might gradually write their way from personal narrative to transpersonal essay. I have not tried to deal with the composing process or with classroom management for writing, important as these are. I took on the assignment about bridging because I think that forcing exposition and argumentation defeats itself and forces out those other kinds of writing that not only lead naturally into essay but that should be fully honored for their own sake. Such development will not only teach thesis writing best but will open up the school writing repertory in sorely needed ways. Formal essay should not be the goal of the writing curriculum, only one outgrowth of it.

[6] *Active Voices IV*, pp. 303–304.

I, YOU, AND IT

Consider, if you will, those primary moments of experience that are necessarily the raw stuff of all discourse. Let us suppose, for example, that I am sitting in a public cafeteria eating lunch. People are arriving and departing, passing through the line, choosing tables, socializing. I am bombarded with smells of food, the sounds of chatter and clatter, the sights of the counter, the tables, the clothing, the faces, the gesticulations and bending of elbows. But I am not just an observer; I am eating and perhaps socializing as well. A lot is going on within me— the tasting and ingesting of the food, reactions to what I observe, emotions about other people. I am registering all these inner and outer stimuli. My perceptual apparatus is recording these moments of raw experience, not in words but in some code of its own that leads to words. This apparatus is somewhat unique to me in the way it selects and ignores stimuli and in the way it immediately connects them with old stimuli and previously formed conceptions. It is difficult to separate this sensory recording from the constant stream of thoughts that is going on simultaneously and parallel to the sensory record but may often depart from it. This verbal stream is the first level of discourse to be considered. The subject is *what is happening now*, and the audience is oneself.

Suppose next that I tell the cafeteria experience to a friend sometime later in conversation. For what reason am I telling him? Would I tell it differently to someone else? Would I tell it differently to the same person at another time and in different circumstances? These are not rhetorical questions but questions about rhetoric. The fact that my account is an unrehearsed, face-to-face vocalization, uttered to *this* person for *this* reason at *this* time and place and in *these* circumstances determines to an enormous degree not only the overall way in which I abstract certain features of the ongoing panorama of the cafeteria scene but also much of the way I choose words, construct sentences, and organize parts. Compare this discourse with the third stage, when

From *College Composition and Communication* Vol. 16, No. 5 (December 1965), 243–48. Copyright © 1965 by the National Council of Teachers of English. Reprinted by permission of the publisher and the author.

my audience is no longer face to face with me, but is farther removed in time and space so that I have to write a letter or memo to him. Informal writing is usually still rather spontaneous, directed at an audience known to the writer, and reflects the transient mood and circumstances in which the writing occurs. Feedback and audience influence, however, are delayed and weakened. Written discourse must replace or compensate for the loss of vocal characteristics and all physical expressiveness of gesture, tone, and manner. Compare in turn now the changes that must occur all down the line when I write about this cafeteria experience in a discourse destined for publication and distribution to a mass, anonymous audience of present and perhaps unborn people. I cannot allude to things and ideas that only my friends know about. I must use a vocabulary, style, logic, and rhetoric that anybody in that mass audience can understand and respond to. I must name and organize what happened during those moments in the cafeteria that day in such a way that this mythical average reader can relate what I say to some primary moments of experience of his own. In other words, whether this published discourse based on the cafeteria luncheon comes out as a fragment of autobiography, a short story, a humorous descriptive essay, or a serious theoretical essay about people's behavior in public places, certain necessities frame the discourse and determine a lot of its qualities before the writer begins to exercise his personal options.

These four stages of discourse—inner verbalization, outer vocalization, correspondence, and formal writing—are of course only the major markers of a continuum that could be much more finely calibrated. This continuum is formed simply by increasing the distance, in all senses, between speaker and audience. The audience is, first, the speaker himself, then another person standing before him, then someone in another time and place but having some personal relation to the speaker, then, lastly, an unknown mass extended over time and space. The activity necessarily changes from thinking to speaking to writing to publishing. (Thinking as inner speech is at least as old as Bergson and William James and as new as Piaget and Vygotsky.) For me no discussion of language, rhetoric, and composition is meaningful except in this context, for there is no speech without a speaker in some relation to a spoken-to and a spoken-about.

Starting with our cafeteria scene again, I would like to trace it as a subject that may be abstracted to any level I would wish. Please understand that by "subject" I mean some primary moments of experience regardless of how dimly they may appear in the discourse. There are four stages in the processing of raw phenomena by the human symbolic apparatus, although, again, one may recognize many gradations in between. This continuum can best be represented by verb tenses, which indicate when events occurred in relation to when the speaker is speaking of them. Suppose I represent the cafeteria scene first as *what is happening*, which would be the lowest level of verbal abstraction of reality: the order and organization of events would correspond most closely to phenomenal reality, and my verbalization of them would be the most immediate and unpondered that is possible. That is, my symbolic representation in this case would entail the least processing of matter by mind. If next I treat the events at the cafeteria as *what happened*, the subject will necessarily partake a little more of my mind and a little less of the original matter. Although the order of events will still be chronological, it is now my memory and not my perceptual apparatus that is doing the selecting. Some things will stick in my mind and some will not, and some things I will choose to retain or reject, depending on which features of this scene and action I wish to bring out. Of the details selected, some I will dwell upon and some I will subordinate considerably. Ideas are mixed with material from the very beginning, but the recollection of a drama—a narrative, that is —inevitably entails more introduction of ideas because this is inherent in the very process of selecting, summarizing, and emphasizing, even if the speaker refrains from commenting directly on the events.

Suppose next that I speak of my cafeteria experience as *what happens*. Obviously, if we consider it for a moment, the difference between *what happened* and *what happens* is not truly a time difference, or at least we must realize that what we are calling a time difference is actually a difference in the level to which I choose to abstract some primary moments of experience. I am now treating my once-upon-a-time interlude at the cafeteria as something that recurs. I have jumped suddenly, it seems, from narrative to generalization. Actually, as we have said, ideas creep in long before this but are hidden in the processing. Now they must be more explicit, for only by renaming the experience and comparing it with other experiences can I present it as what happens. No primary moments of experience recur. What we mean is that we as observers see similarities in different experiences. Only the human mind, capable of sorting and classifying reality, can do this. What I do, for example, is make an analogy between something in the cafeteria experience and something I singled out of a number of other experiences. I summarize a lot of little formless dramas into pointed narratives and then I put these narratives into some classes, which I and others before me have created. In this third stage of processing, then, the cafeteria scene will become a mere example, among several others, of some general statement such as "The food you get in restaurants is not as good as what you get at home," or "People don't like me," or "Americans do not socialize as readily with strangers in public places as Italians do," or "The arrivals and departures within a continuous group create changes in excitation level comparable to the raising and lowering of electric potential in variously stimulated sensory receptors." It is apparent that these sample generalizations could all have contained the cafeteria experience as an example but vary a great deal in their abstractness, their range of applicability, their objectivity or universal truth value, and their originality.

The transition from a chronological to an analogical discourse is of enormous importance in teaching. The student must forsake the given order of time and replace it with an order of ideas. To do this he must summarize drastically the original primary moments of experience, find classes of inclusion and exclusion, and rename the moments so that it becomes clear how they are alike or different. Most students fail to create original and interesting classes because they are unwittingly encouraged to borrow their generalizations from old slogans, wise saws, reference books, and teachers' essay questions, instead of having to forge them from their own experience. Many students leave out the illustrations completely and offer only their apparently source-less opinions. Others, reluctant to leave the haven of narrative, tell several anecdotes and never show how they are related. But these are failures of teachers, not of students. Proper writing assignments can lead the students to good generalizations.

In what I will call the last stage of symbolizing a subject, you may wonder why I still refer to the cafeteria, since none of that experience appears any longer in the discourse, which is now a highly theoretical essay. That is deceptive; it is behind the discourse, buried in the processing and so combined with other experiences, and so renamed, that we do not recognize it any more. The "subject" seems to be a theory, some combining and developing of generalizations. This stage is telling *what will, may,* or *could happen.* Some general assertions previously arrived at by analogical thinking are now plugged into each other in various ways according to the rules of formal logic. Suppose we take some generalizations about the behavior of Americans and the behavior of Italians and the behavior of South Sea islanders and we transform and combine these statements in such a way as to come out with an anthropological conclusion that was not evident in any of the original moments of experience nor even in the generalizations about them. It took manipulations of logic to show the implications of the earlier statements. To go beyond this stage is to enter the realm of mathematical equations. What will, may, or could happen is a high-level inference entailing tautology, verbal equations. My own essay is an example of stage-four abstraction. I am setting up a series of equations among "levels of abstraction," "distance between speaker, listener, and subject," verb tenses, human faculties, and kinds of logic. I will then conclude a theory about composition curriculum by combining generalizations about what happens in discourse with what happens in the learning process of people. What enables me to do this is that something fundamental to the operation of our nervous system underlies all these man-made conceptions.

I have traced separately, and grossly, two abstractive progressions —one in which the speaker's audience becomes more remote and diffused over time and space, and another in which the speaker's subject becomes less and less matter and more and more idea. Each relation —and of course the two must be taken together—entails certain necessities, and shifts in these relations entail changes all down the line, from the organization of the whole discourse to individual word choice. As we move through the progressions, perception gives way to memory and memory to ratiocination; chronology gives way to analogy and analogy to tautology. But each faculty and kind of logic depends on the one before. In view of what we know now about abstractive processes and the cognitive and verbal growth of children, this order seems pedagogically sound to me. In other words, the necessities inherent in devising a rhetoric for an increasingly remote audience and in abstracting moments of experience to higher and higher symbolic levels are precisely the limitations which should shape our writing assignments.

According to Piaget, and Vygotsky agrees with him, the early egocentric speech of the child becomes gradually "socialized" and adapts itself to other people. At the same time his mental outlook decenters; that is, he gradually yields up his initial, emotionally preferred vantage point, and expands his perspective so as to include many other points of view. Of course, both these kinds of growth never really stop. The movement is from self to world, from a point to an area, from a private world of egocentric chatter to a public universe of discourse. Cognitively, the young person passes through, according to Jerome Bruner, three phases—the enactive, the iconic, and the symbolic. First he knows things by manipulating them with his hands, then he begins to classify and interpret the world by means of image summaries, and finally he can carry out logical operations in his head modeled on his earlier physical manipulations. Most teachers have always known that in some way the child should move from the concrete to the abstract, but the whole notion of an abstraction scale has never been clear and still requires more study. I have found the communication engineers' definition of coding to be very helpful in all this: Coding is the substitution of one set of events for another. What I call the processing of matter by mind is in fact the substitution of inner events for outer events. These inner events are neural, and we don't yet know very much about them. We can be sure, however, that as the child's nervous system develops, these neural operations become more complicated. A series of writing assignments is a series of thinking assignments and therefore a sequence of internal operations.

As a model for a composition course, imagine the trinity of discourse—first, second, and third persons—to be a single circle that separates into three overlapping circles which move out until they merely touch. The discourse unity of somebody talking to somebody else about something is what we must never lose, but we can create phases, not by decomposing composition into analytical elements but by gradually pushing the persons apart. Language and rhetoric are variable factors of each other and of shifting relations among persons. We abstract not only from something but for someone. Rhetoric, on the other hand, is to some extent dictated by the abstraction level we have chosen; in drama and narrative one appeals mainly by concrete recognitions, and in exposition and argumentation mainly by one's classes and logical justice. So the rationale of our composition course lies in some crossing of the two progressions I have sketched. This is not only possible but will spiral the curriculum. For example, we ask the student to tell what happened in four different rhetorics—to himself as he spontaneously recalls a memory, to a friend face to face, to someone he knows in a letter, and to the world at large in formal writing. Generalizations and theories can be dealt with first in interior monologues, then in dialogues, in letters and diaries, and only at the end in essays. The student is never assigned a subject, only a form and the forms are ordered according to the preceding ideas, as they seem to apply to individuals.

Specifically, I would have the student write in this order: all kinds of real and invented interior monologues, dramatic monologues, dialogues, plays, letters, diaries, fragments of autobiography, eye-witness accounts, reporters-at-large (modeled on those in *The New Yorker*), case studies, first- and third-person fiction, essays of generalization and essays of logical argumentation. Many teachers may feel that such a program slights exposition in favor of so-called personal or creative writing. In the first place, one doesn't learn exposition just by writing it all the time. An enormous amount of other learning must take place before one can write worthwhile essays of ideas; that is in the nature of the whole abstraction process. All writing teaches exposition. Furthermore, I cannot conceive a kind of discourse which does not contain ideas; even in concrete description, contrasts, similarities, and notions of causality and progression are strongly implicit. Monologues, dialogues, letters, diaries, and narratives may either contain explicit ideas or be shaped by ideas. What do we mean by a *pointed* narrative? What are Socratic dialogues about? And why do we have students digging for meaning in literary works of imagination if they are not full of ideas? The issue is not idea writing versus other kinds of writing but rather which *form* the ideas are presented in. All modes must be taught. The panic to teach exposition is partly responsible for its being taught so badly. Teachers do not feel they can take the time to let a student abstract from the ground up. But if they do not, he will never learn to write exposition.

There are several corollaries of the program I am proposing. Since it attempts to exercise the student in all possible relations that might obtain between him and an audience and a subject, one corollary is that he not be allowed to get stuck with one audience or at one range of the abstractive spectrum. It is essential that he address someone besides the English teacher and get some kind of feedback other than red marks. As one solution, I suggest that he be accustomed to write to the class peers as being the nearest thing to a contemporary world at large. Compositions should be read in class, and out of class, reacted to and discussed. One must know the effects of one's rhetoric on someone who does not give grades and does not stand as an authority figure. I suggest also the performance and publication of student works as frequently as possible. Monologues, dialogues, letters, and diaries give the student the opportunity both to address a real or invented person outside the classroom and to adopt a voice not his own.

What most frequently freezes the student at one end of the abstractive spectrum is too much writing about reading. Perhaps because of the great influence of college essay exams and of literary exegesis, composition courses often boil down to "how to write about books." This is a narrow notion of exposition. Abstracting about someone else's already high abstraction, whether it be a book or a teacher's essay question, means that certain essential issues of choice about selecting and treating material and creating classes are never permitted to come up for the student. When I assign a topic such as "loyalty" or "Irony in A. E. Housman," all I am asking the student to do is to find illustrations for my classifications. By doing half of his work for him, I am impoverishing his education. Rather than assign literary exegesis, I would have him write in the forms he reads. As practitioner he will naturally be a better literary critic than a student who only analyzes. Rather than assign book reports and essays on books, I would encourage the student to incorporate into his essays of generalization illustrations and ideas drawn from his reading and to mix these with his own experiences and observations; in other words, get *him* to create the classes into which he can fit people and actions drawn from both books and life. There is a real place for reading in a composition course, not as subject matter to write about but as a source of experience and as a repertory of discourse. After all, reading provides some excellent primary moments of experience.

From the perceptual level on up the student should be forced in effect to confront all the right issues of choice. Only in this way will he develop the faculties necessary to produce the ideas of exposition. On the same grounds, I am leery of asking the student to read about writing. I have spent a lot of time unteaching the dicta of composition texts and manuals of advice. Trial and error best develops judgment and taste, if this trial and error process is keyed in with the student's learning schedule. Explanations and definitions of good style, technique, and rhetoric create more problems than they solve. The issue here is not only one of cognitive development but of psychological independence. We must give students an emotional mandate to play the symbolic scale, to find subjects and shape them, to invent ways to act upon others, and to discover their own voice.